THE DIRECT METHOD

Adam Hamadache

First published in 2018 by DHM (www.dhm.agency)

For Katie

Your understanding, your support and your love makes life a joy and succeeding in business a doddle.

Connect with Adam Hamadache:

Email:
adam@dhm.agency

LinkedIn:
www.linkedin.com/in/adamhamadache

Websites:
www.dhm.agency
www.thedirectmethod.com

Contents

Chapter 1

Introduction

In 2008, my career in hotel marketing started and I've been studying and practicing it ever since. As I write this in 2018, the hotel industry has changed enormously – and this statement is most pertinent in the ways in which hotel guests are deciding upon and booking their leisure breaks. If you're a hotelier, I won't need to explain how the online travel agents (OTAs) have come to dominate the booking-decision process in recent years, nor is it necessary to explain at length the sky-high commission levels being charged to hotels. Now whether OTAs are ethically and morally right in charging in excess of 18% to hotels for each booking is a debate beyond the scope of this book. Rather, as someone who has dedicated the last decade to learning and implementing hotel marketing strategy to encourage bookings direct, one thing has become crystal clear: **there is another way.**

Why read this book?

In case this is the first time you've come into contact with me, or one of my businesses, let me briefly explain why I've come to believe this statement, and why I'm qualified to advise and discuss this topic of 'direct bookings' at length. First and foremost, I'm the Founder and CEO of a UK-based digital marketing agency exclusively for unbranded hotels. DHM (which stands for Direct Hotel Marketing) works with over 30 independent hotels to implement marketing strategy that helps to improve sales and reduce commission. In 2017, along with our sister agency (which has nothing to do with hotels, but rather digital marketing in general) our team were awarded the Global Award for Growing Businesses Online by Google in New York. Our companies beat off 1,100 marketing agencies from 58 countries to take Google's biggest honour for marketing agencies. That was a good day in business.

I'm also the Associate Director of an independent hotel called the Cranleigh Boutique in the Lake District. Our little 23-bedroom hotel has in the past beat travel giants P&O Ferries and Bournemouth Tourism to the Best Use of Social Media award at the Travel Marketing Awards and, more significantly, commands approx. 96% of its bookings direct with an occupancy percentage sitting neatly in the high 80s. Lastly, we've managed to grow our social media following to over 250,000+ Facebook likes – that's more than The Dorchester, The Savoy and The Ritz combined.

Whilst these accolades read well, they don't tell the full story. It was Thomas Edison who famously said, 'I haven't failed, I've just found 10,000 ways that didn't work.' Whilst 10,000 would be pushing it, the route to developing The Direct Method has been laden with unsuccessful (and often expensive!) ideas and strategies that haven't quite hit the mark. To add to this complexity, the things we've found to have worked well a few years ago are less effective today; such is the fast-moving pace of the digital world.

Who is The Direct Method for?

What's presented in these pages is a collection of principles; proven approaches that have been honed and refined over time. Moreover, they have been tested and proven to have worked effectively across the broad spectrum of hotel styles. Quirky urban 20-bedroom boutiques, 100-bedroom golf and spa resorts and 40-bedroom traditional country house hotels have all seen positive results from The Direct Method. Regardless of the star-rating, the location, the size or the style of your hotel, The Direct Method provides a set of principles to how your marketing strategy can and should be implemented. What will inevitably differ is the message and style of how these principles are applied. The formality of the tone of voice, the style of the images, the backing music of the videography, the target audience and countless other aspects all make up the variables of how The Direct Method can be applied. When working with a new client at DHM, half the challenge is understanding how best to apply these principles. In short, The Direct Method, whilst applicable to almost any hotel is by no means a one-size fits all – it provides a framework, or a skeleton of ideas with which the marketing messages can be added to flesh out the overall strategy.

Furthermore, The Direct Method fundamentally is about driving more leisure bookings into your hotel. The main reason for this is that encouraging corporate travellers to book direct can be a bit like pushing water uphill. More often than not corporate bookers are required by their respective companies to book via an OTA like Booking.com or the Global Distribution System (GDS). No amount of clever marketing is going to encourage corporate travellers to book direct with your hotel en masse so we don't try. Where The Direct Method works best is for those guests looking for an 'experience' not just a bed. I'm referring to the short-breakers, the couple who visit a hotel for a couple of days to get away from it all, or to celebrate a special occasion like a birthday or an anniversary. To put it another way, guests looking for a 'bed' are those who opt for

Travelodge or Premier Inn in the UK – the two biggest hotel chains that offer a high-quality standardised product, usually in a central location at an affordable price. These guests mostly aren't looking to spend an awful lot of time in the hotel, rather to use it as a base to explore or simply somewhere to sleep after attending an event. If you have a hotel that specialises in offering guests an experience, The Prospect Method and The Browser Method are for you.

Defining the Terms

The Direct Method is made up of three parts: Prospects, Browsers and Weddings. For years at DHM we approached our marketing by focusing on the channel and the message. A hotel would approach us and ask us if we could manage their social media or run their email campaigns. We'd say yes and get to work on understanding their business and how best to speak to their customers, crafting clever messages to create engagement. In truth, the results would be varied. More often than not, we'd get it spot on and the hoteliers would be astounded at how a simple email campaign crafted in a certain way could produce in excess of £10,000 in room sales when the most they'd ever managed was £2,000 when doing it themselves. Other times, for the best will in the world, our campaigns would fall flat and send us back to the drawing board to start again with a new approach. Over time we've come to realise that rather than starting with a channel or a message, a successful marketing strategy must start with the customer and the relationship they have with the hotel.

The Prospect who had a superb stay at your hotel two years ago, who subscribes to your emails and follows you on social media channels needs a completely different set of marketing messages to the Browser who has stumbled across your website whilst actively searching for a 3-night break next month to celebrate an anniversary with their partner. Furthermore, the excited bride-to-be who is searching for her dream wedding venue needs a different set of messages again, not only because her needs are far different from the other two, but because the booking process for a wedding is substantially different to the booking process for accommodation. At its core, The Direct Method is about shaping the marketing channels and messages to suit the customer, as opposed to thinking about who you want to target on social media or what you think your email database wants to hear about.

This book is not about eradicating the OTAs out of your business altogether: rather on one hand it offers a marketing strategy refined over time to reduce commission and ensure your hotel maximises its direct bookings, and on the other hand offers a unique marketing system to deliver warmed-up wedding enquiries and viewings that can be converted into more wedding bookings by your hotel's sales team.

My hope is that the tools and techniques described in these pages enlighten you as to how even the smallest hotels can compete with the powerhouses of the global OTAs. There will inevitably be parts of The Direct Method that you already have in place, being implemented either by your own team or by an agency or consultant – I implore you not to skip these parts of the book as often they can offer the most insight. The smallest of tweaks in marketing approaches, I've come to realise, can yield the biggest difference in results. Furthermore, I encourage you to explore this book with an open-mind; I've lost count of the times I've had a hotelier who was sceptical of our methods only to have them admit joyfully they were pleased they gave it a chance.

I wish you every success on your journey to take control back from the OTAs and substantially grow the profitability of your hotel. I truly hope you see the logic and the benefit of The Direct Method and see what I've come to learn about hotel marketing; there really is another way.

> Take our online assessment now to understand how your hotel rates on our hotel marketing scale. Visit www.thedirectmethod.com

Part One

The Prospect Method

Chapter 2

The Prospect Method: Introduction

A Prospect can be defined as someone who knows, likes and trusts your business. They have come into contact with your hotel in some fashion and now know the general gist of what you're about, where you're located and what you offer to your guests.

A Prospect may have stayed with you in the past and enjoyed their stay. They may have attended a wedding at your hotel and were impressed with the venue, food and service offered on the day. Equally, a Prospect may be someone who has, in the past, visited your website and subscribed to your email database or may have liked or followed your Facebook page or Instagram account. In short, a Prospect has in some way come into contact with your hotel and liked what they've seen.

For all intents and purposes your Prospects are your hotel's lowest hanging fruit for bookings. The challenging thing about Prospects, though, is that they're unlikely to be actively looking for a hotel stay right now. You can turn up in their inbox, on their Facebook wall and on their Instagram stream but they will need a good amount of persuading to convince them to book. That said, true Prospects can represent a considerable amount of income if marketed to correctly. They after all, by definition, think your hotel is great and would probably give genuine consideration to a sales offer if it was communicated in the right ways.

This is called The Prospect Method. It is a formula for encouraging those people who know, like and trust your hotel to take action and make a booking. It consists of four key strands: data capturing the Prospect's information; nurturing and building the relationship with them; remarketing to them and, most significantly, creating a buying environment that will encourage them to book.

This chapter will show you the method we use at DHM to drive more Prospects into your business and importantly, to encourage those bookings direct.

Chapter 3

The Prospect Method: Data Capture

When you think about it, hotels are in a privileged position when it comes to data. Over the years DHM has worked with restaurants and bars and the job of capturing data is notoriously more difficult in these businesses because the transactions often don't require the customer to part with any data. Hotels, of course, are different. Most hotels will require you to part with your email address, postal address, telephone number and more, making it easy to build a list of customer data quickly.

The GDPR (General Data Protection Regulation) which came into effect on May 25th 2018 for all businesses trading with European Union citizens (whether located in the EU or not) requires any business to obtain unambiguous consent from any customer whose information they wish to use to market their services. This regulation is wide and varied and goes well beyond the scope of this book. Suffice to say that this chapter assumes that any and all data acquired for the purposes of marketing your hotel's services is obtained in a manner which is compliant with this regulation.

> For more information on how GDPR affects your hotel's marketing, you can download our tips sheet at www.dhm.agency/gdpr

On the whole, in my experience hotels don't capture data well. Or if they do, many aren't using it to their full advantage. More times than I can remember, I've stayed at a hotel on a leisure break and I've never heard from that property again, despite being very willing to receive their communications long after I've stayed. All too often hotel guests utter the words, 'What was the name of that lovely hotel we stayed in last year?' If you've worked on delivering a remarkable experience to guests but haven't stayed in touch either via email, social media or otherwise, it is highly likely that your customers will forget the name of your hotel, irrespective of how great their stay was. When this happens, it's a complete failure on the hotel's part – those Prospects, who may well have been willing to engage in future offers and communications, will never stay or even consider staying again owing to the fact that they can't even remember the name of the hotel!

Now, of course, encouraging repeat business from guests is almost always dependent on the type of hotel you run and the type of stay the guest is looking for. A couple that need a 'bed' for the night as they have an event or something specific in the local area to attend i.e. a wedding, an award ceremony, etc. have probably been motivated to choose your hotel because of your location and price. On the other hand, a couple looking for an 'experience' tend not to be as motivated by location or price. They have chosen your property because of the facilities, the brand credentials, the star rating (not that most customers know the difference between a 4-red star hotel and 5-star guest accommodation but that's a separate issue!) and perhaps secondary to these points, the price and location. In short, the latter couple are probably looking to spend a considerable amount of time in the hotel, the former couple are looking to sleep, eat and leave.

It's the 'experience' couple that offers the highest chance of repeat custom and it's these 'Prospects' who you must stay in touch with across as many channels as is appropriate to a) remind them that you exist and b) encourage them to return at some point in the future.

Social Login Wi-Fi

One of the easiest ways to capture this data of your customers (and let it be said that you don't just want one email address per couple; ideally you want both) is by using a Social Login Wi-Fi tool.

These typically are very easy to set up, inexpensive to run and will ensure that you maximise the amount of consented data coming into your business. If you're not familiar with the term, you'll probably have experienced it somewhere in a hotel, bar or café. When you attempt to access the Internet, you are met with a branded pop-up screen requesting you to login via a social channel or an email address to access the Wi-Fi network.

On the whole our experience of this tool is extremely positive and allows you to not only quickly and efficiently collect customer email addresses, but also a great deal more information should they choose to login via Facebook, Instagram or Twitter.

This method of data capture is particularly useful in obtaining the data of non-resident diners or wedding guests, from whom it would otherwise be more difficult to acquire data.

> For more information about our preferred suppliers of Social Login Wi-Fi solutions visit www.dhm.agency/suppliers

Facebook Competitions

Another traditional way of capturing Prospect data is to run a competition on a platform like Facebook. Now competition data is notorious at being relatively low quality given that it encourages Prospects who have neither the inclination nor the income level to invest in your hotel's services. That said, it's still a viable way of reaching a wider audience and starting the nurturing process with Prospects who may visit your hotel sometime in the future.

Facebook competitions are importantly a good means of turning a 'like' into a 'subscriber'. That is, encouraging someone who has liked your Facebook page to submit their email address to subscribe to your email marketing. It's also a great way of obtaining more specific information such as birthday, anniversary (if applicable) and partner's birthday. Whenever we run a Facebook competition for a hotel, it is imperative to ask for these three special occasion dates (although never as a required field and avoid asking for the year, just month and date will suffice). The reason for this (if it's not obvious) is because these are the three times of the year that a Prospect is most likely to visit a hotel for an 'experience' stay. Capturing this information will allow you to automate emails to these Prospects a few weeks prior to their special occasion, making sure you've turned up on their radar at a time of year when they are most receptive to a hotel's marketing messages.

When running a competition, be it via Facebook or otherwise, make the prize as attractive as possible. Big prizes command attention and in some cases, it can earn you some solid press coverage. All too often at DHM we see hotels making a big song and dance about winning a 2-night break. Whilst that in principle is not a bad prize, it won't get people talking and engaging in your product (which, by the way, is one of the main reasons you'd want to run a competition in the first place).

At the Cranleigh Boutique, we ran a competition to win the entire hotel for the weekend. To our knowledge it was the first time a hotel in the UK had done it and whilst at the time we only had 19 bedrooms, it was this audacious prize that got people talking, liking our Facebook page and plenty of press coverage in publications suited to our target demographic. Not to mention, of course, the thousands upon thousands of entrants whose data we had collected and countless others who browsed through our website to get a feel for our hotel and what was on offer.

Importantly, the prize was only redeemable over the quieter winter months where occupancy is typically low regardless of how much marketing is done. What was lost in sales for those prize nights, was gained ten-fold in a wave of Prospects who started to know, like and trust our product.

Why Bother with Social Media?

I've always seen social media as a noncommittal first step to find out more about a business, or a noncommittal next step to have that business stay in touch after a purchase. As you will no doubt be aware the key fact is that social media is noncommittal – it doesn't mean much when a Prospect likes your Facebook page or follows your Instagram account. Likes and follows are, on the whole, given all too easily and regularly rendering them near on meaningless in encouraging Prospects to engage in your property.

In somewhat contradictory fashion to the previous statement, at DHM and the Cranleigh Boutique, we put an enormous amount of emphasis on the importance of social media as a means to engage with Prospects, but there's one very clear objective to our work: get the Prospect to take their commitment further by sharing their email address.

Email is (by some margin) a much better medium to encourage genuine and real engagement with your property. Primarily because there are far fewer distractions in an email inbox than on a social channel. At the time of writing, the Facebook dashboard shows a list of online friends on the right-hand side as well as offering a never-ending stream of content that is seemingly more interesting than the last.

Email on the other hand (in most interfaces) requires the user to open the email, then engage with it with minimal screen distraction and often click a link to find out more. This makes the medium of email a far better channel to have a sales conversation.

To put it another way, if email is the equivalent to providing a sales presentation in a quiet boardroom in front of a projector displaying beautiful imagery of your hotel, social media would be like trying to deliver the same sales presentation in a noisy café with videos of friends' new born babies and old school friends' wedding photos flicking across the screen behind you. No matter how lovely your hotel, or how captivating your message, you can't compete with cute babies and gossip, so don't try.

Chapter 4

The Prospect Method: Remarketing

Imagine a packed Wembley Stadium filled with your Prospects. That's 90,000 people who have at the very least visited your website for a few minutes all the way through to the people who have stayed with you three or four times – and everyone in between. In short, anyone who has come into contact with your hotel in the last 18 months with a view to booking a room. Now imagine that the advertising boards all the way around the stadium are your ads focusing on your unique selling points, and the benefits of booking direct. The cost for this is approx. £300. Would you do it?

If the answer is no, then the Direct Method for all its proven benefits won't help you to get more direct bookings!

Hopefully you can see that this would be a complete no-brainer. This analogy (short of your Prospects actually sitting in a stadium together) is precisely what Google Remarketing allows you to do.

For the unacquainted, one can advertise on Google a multitude of ways. Most think that 'search' is the only platform in the hotel industry, which is the process of bidding on keywords (or search terms) to have your text ad appear at the top of Google. To use a basic example, when someone types in 'hotels in London' and you're bidding on that keyword, your ad may appear, and you only pay when a user clicks on your ad. Hence the term pay-per-click.

Effective use of this form of advertising is a complex, ever-changing science and must be managed very carefully to create return on investment. Done incorrectly by someone who is inexperienced in Google AdWords can be a very fast way to lose a lot of money. (I'm proud to say that the wider DHM team are one of the best at it, winning the Google Global Award for Growing Businesses Online in New York in 2017, beating 1,100 marketing agencies from 58 countries to the top prize, but I digress!)

Another form of advertising is to run image or animated ads across Google's 'display network' which is literally a selection of billions of ad spaces across millions of websites across the Internet. Any ad you see with a little triangle and an 'x' in the top right-hand corner of the ad is a Google Remarketing ad.

The difference is that these ads have nothing to do with the user visiting Google.com and everything to do with them visiting your website. The technical term is to 'drop a cookie on their web browser'. This allows your ads to 'follow' the user around the

Internet for a period of up to 540 days or approx. 18 months. The most beautiful part is that it is incredibly cheap. Depending on the amount of traffic your website receives, you will be unlikely to exceed £25 per month on this form of advertising. For this investment, you'll likely be advertising 20,000-30,000 times ONLY to the people that have visited your website.

In my experience, the average number of website unique users is 5,000 per month for an independent hotel. If you have Google Remarketing running for the maximum cookie duration of 540 days (18 months) then after this time, you will have approx. 90,000 unique individuals (neatly the exact capacity of Wembley Stadium) seeing your ads at a cost of £25 per month.

It gets better though. More often than not if you set up a new Google AdWords account, you will receive £75 worth of free credit after spending an initial £25 – so your year one cost is more likely to be £225.

Whilst anyone can see that this form of advertising represents high value for the volume of targeted Prospects you can get in front of, I would argue that the most important reason your hotel should be using it is because in the last decade of my hotel marketing experience, I can honestly say I've come across fewer than 10 hotels that are running Google

Remarketing campaigns to good effect. This form of advertising is so underused in our industry which means that your hotel would have a distinct advantage over your competitors and the OTAs (Online Travel Agents) by using it.

One of the core benefits of Google Remarketing is that you can advertise (for free!) on some of the largest websites in the world, often on the front page of these websites. For years I've been using GoodHousekeeping.co.uk as a perfect example as the ad space on the front page of their website is four or five times bigger than the Good Housekeeping logo! Hotels are often stunned to see how my DHM ad is sat pride of place on such a prestigious website, smack-bang in the middle of the page. The next time you see a Booking.com ad following you around whilst you're browsing the Internet (perhaps remarketing your own hotel back at you), remember that it's not their deep pockets that allows them to do it. And let's face it, Booking.com are the experts at selling hotel rooms – they sell more than anyone else in the world – if they're using remarketing, your hotel probably should too.

The Different Types of Remarketing

So far Google Remarketing has been explained but there are actually a few types to be aware of. Namely the Facebook and YouTube equivalents. Facebook remarketing (or retargeting as they refer to it) works in the same way as Google but the ads are shown across Facebook and Instagram only, and across multiple devices. So, if you visit a hotel's website on your mobile phone and they have Facebook retargeting set up and you are logged into Facebook in the background, those ads will be fed to you on Facebook and Instagram on your tablet, desktop or whatever device you happen to be looking at Facebook or Instagram on. Often this process is scarily quick: you could look at something on your computer at work and 20 minutes later see the ad show on your phone when scrolling through the Facebook or Instagram apps.

YouTube remarketing provides the platform for video remarketing ads. There's lots of ways this can work but probably the most recognisable is the ads that appear with a mandatory five second watch before the chosen video starts. Fascinatingly, at the time of writing, those first five seconds before the user can skip the ad are free. In fact, the first 29 seconds are free, you (as the advertiser) only pay if the user watches 30 seconds or more, or if they click on the ad. Done effectively over time, you can achieve tens of thousands of video ad views for a few hundred pounds.

How Does Remarketing Help to Nurture Prospects?

'The merits of remarketing are great' you may be thinking, but how does it help to nurture (and ultimately sell to) Prospects? Because as the saying goes, the worst number in marketing is one. Send a Prospect a marketing message once and it's too easy to ignore. Follow up (in the right ways) multiple times, they are more likely to engage in your business. You want to stay front of mind for your Prospects when they are in the market for a hotel break, and there's no cheaper, more effective, unobtrusive medium than remarketing ads to do that.

Chapter 5

The Prospect Method: Nurture

The whole concept of 'nurturing' your customers is an essential part of the relationship building and maintaining process. It's the messages you send via email, the photos and videos posted to social media websites and the descriptive copy explaining what you do on your website; as long as there is no overt sales message, it can be considered nurturing content as it is serving to inform the Prospect about your services.

The 55/6 Rule

The 55/6 rule is something we've come to perfect within DHM and it essentially works by nurturing for 55 days and selling for 6 days. Typically, most hotels don't split their communications, attempting to do both simultaneously, serving neither to effectively nurture the Prospect nor to effectively sell to them. This is usually evident in a monthly or bi-monthly 'newsletter' email which tries to cram in as much information as it possibly can, as well as burying a special offer in there too. All too often, the result is that most Prospects don't read any or all of it, missing the offer.

The 55/6 rule approaches it very differently. Whether you are sending an email or posting to social media, it's almost always better to only say one thing, and say that one thing well. In this case, when aiming to send a nurture email, you should absolutely never include a sales offer.

The same is true for the 6 days of selling. When looking to sell, create a big song and dance about the special offer you are promoting. It's important not to overdo this though – we've all been subscribed to hotels or perhaps other types of businesses where all they do is send offer emails. That's why we advise working on these 61-day cycles, so that every two months a sales campaign is launched before reverting communications back to nurturing again.

By adopting the 55/6 rule in your hotel, you'll quickly find that your content plan can be easily mapped out, serving to countdown until the next 'sales window'. Of course, it's not as if you will only sell rooms on these 6 days every 2 months, far from it, but remember this strategy is designed purely for Prospects – people that know, like and trust your business already that aren't necessarily actively looking for a stay. A good 55 days of nurturing will set the scene nicely to create the right buying environment for some of these Prospects to get off auto-pilot and engage with your business fully.

Email Nurturing

Your nurture emails must never, ever have a sales message in them. My team and I have had countless conversations with clients who ask, 'Could I just slip a special offer into that email?' Our response is always the same: only if you want to be known as a hotel that's always sending sales emails. This isn't our team being difficult, it's our years of experience of knowing what works and what doesn't.

A good example of a nurture email is the 'thank you' email. A simple, authentic email from the General Manager or owner of the property conveying their gratitude that you (the Prospect) have either stayed with the hotel in the past or have chosen to be a subscriber of the emails. All it needs to be is a few sentences long, with a quick 'PS' asking the recipient to reply should they wish to provide any feedback directly to the GM/owner – good or bad.

Most businesses never do this. Almost never do you see a hotel doing this (unless of course it's one of our clients) and yet it can be so powerful. It's quick to read, it's saying one thing and saying it well, and it's not asking for anything in return from the recipient. Moreover, the 'PS' at the end of the email can be a really clever way to get further engagement from the Prospect. If a particular Prospect has spent five or six minutes replying to the GM/owner about how lovely their stay was last year and thanking them for the email (this happens a great deal when you send this kind of email) that particular Prospect is going to be much more likely to engage with future emails because they've just spent five minutes reliving their experience in their own mind.

Another type of nurture email might be the 'What's on' email, listing a variety of upcoming events within the hotel, as well any notable local events worthy of communicating.

Staff spotlight emails can be really powerful at nurturing Prospects too as they can make your hotel look and feel more personable. Over the years we've spotlighted receptionists who've been with the hotel for over 20 years, Michelin trained chefs and owners or General Managers who wish to convey their vision for the hotel.

Social Nurturing

In January 2018, Facebook made a change to its algorithm that was significant to anyone managing a Facebook business page. Essentially the change means that only people that have actively engaged with your content or your pages will be fed these posts in their newsfeed. It's an attempt by Facebook to a) feed its users what it believes to be more relevant content, but also b) get you to use its advertising tool if you want to reach all of your followers.

> For the most up to date changes to Facebook and how it affects your hotel, visit
> www.dhm.agency/blog

This change aside, video is key to mastering Facebook. Dozens of 45-75-second videos focusing on one area you want to promote. Weddings, each individual room type (each individual room if necessary), conference space, food and beverage etc. The idea is to say one thing and say it well. For a more detailed overview of how to best use video to promote your hotel, visit the Impressive Content chapter on page xx.

Countdown

By adopting the 55/6 rule, you can begin to get your Prospects excited about the next sales campaign by effectively counting down the days, hours and minutes until the next campaign begins. If nothing else, your nurturing content during the 55 days must grab the Prospect's attention and a content strategy focused around a date in the future can create sufficient intrigue for the Prospect to learn more. This can be done using a variety of images, video and text across your social media channels, as well as using ticking-timer widgets like tickcounter.com where you can create a custom countdown timer and embed into emails.

When posting content of this nature on social media, be sure to post a link to encourage your Prospects to subscribe to your email list – the forthcoming flash sales must be reserved exclusively for your email subscribers. The reason for this is

a. you want to encourage your social followers to engage with you on multiple levels – this will in turn increase their engagement in your hotel. It's all too easy to follow a business on Facebook and ignore everything they post but if you follow on Facebook and subscribe to their emails, and the content carries a consistent theme then it becomes harder to ignore.

b. Email is a far better medium to sell on given the world of distractions present on social media channels

c. Before any Prospect commits to even considering booking a stay at your property, they need to take a series of small actions. An important small action is to subscribe to the email database. The more small actions you can encourage before you open up the sales campaign, the more likely they'll be to engage with the sales message.

Chapter 6

The Prospect Method: Create a Buying Environment

What Most Hotels Do When They Sell

When it comes to using email marketing to sell special offers, most hotels will send one email. They'll create a brilliant offer, feature it in the monthly 'newsletter' email, be a little vague about the call-to-action and hope for the best. Given the industry open rate average for emails is approximately 20%, the other 80% won't even open the email to understand what the offer is. If the sales offer is buried somewhere within the long email, it's fair to say that a good chunk of the 20% that do open the email won't actually see the offer. For the vast minority that do actually see the offer and read it, even if it's an earth-shatteringly great deal, if the recipient isn't thinking about a hotel stay in the first place, there's a very good chance they'll simply just ignore it.

Of the now (probably miniscule) that open the email, see and read the offer, and are in the frame of mind to consider a hotel stay, there will inevitably be a fair proportion that get distracted and forget about it. Or perhaps they like what they see, but it's just an inconvenient time and therefore don't take action.

My point, of course, with all of this is that burying a sales message in a long email newsletter and sending it once will not produce a high level of revenue given the vast majority of recipients won't see it nor engage with the message long enough to give it the full consideration it deserves. This example is a perfect illustration of throwing out a sales message without having done the work to create a buying environment.

How to Create a Buying Environment

A buying environment creates anticipation, excitement and compels the Prospect to take action for fear of missing out. The previous example was a whisper in a very noisy world of marketing messages. Unless, as a Prospect, you read the offer at the right time and it was perfectly priced you're unlikely to take action.

In recent years, deal websites like Travelzoo and Secret Escapes have been incredibly successful as they create great buying environments for customers. They offer high value deals with a specific deadline with only a scarce number of deals available. They tease a 'from price' which may only represent a small percentage of the prices available to lure you in and encourage you to engage further with the offer. In short, they use urgency and scarcity to prompt action. It is not uncommon for a hotel to create a high value deal, promote it on a website like Travelzoo and sell 300 room nights in a few weeks. The big problem with doing this, of course, is whilst you are driving strong revenue into the business, you are probably offering a considerable discount on rack rates AND paying above 20% in commission. The Prospect Method is all about creating your own deal with your own group of Prospects, replicating the techniques used by these successful deal websites and not succumbing to the often necessity of slicing two-thirds or half of the profit from a booking by having to pay large sums in commission.

With this in mind, first we have to adopt the Steve Jobs iPhone technique. The now iconic presentation featuring the late CEO of Apple presenting the iPhone in his synonymous black turtle-neck jumper prompted thousands of Apple customers to queue up overnight (and for over a week in some cases!) so they could get their hands on the highly anticipated iPhone. He achieved this by effectively teasing the product, building excitement and making customers wait. This 'teasing' is precisely what we want to do to your email list to ensure that we get a figurative queue of Prospects lining up to buy your upcoming special offer. This 'tease' will be broadcast explaining that a special offer is launching tomorrow at a specific time. The details of this offer are secret and can't be shared until it opens but what can be assured is that it is one of the best deals ever made available to our Prospects and it is not to be missed.

Now the tone of voice and use of hyperbolic statements need to be adjusted to suit the style of your hotel and the offer being presented but the key is to build excitement.

> To view and download an example template of the 'tease, offer, follow up' campaign visit www.dhm.agency/templates

What we're wanting to do here is build suspense and curiosity in your Prospect's mind so that when the offer is officially launched and lands in the Prospect's inbox the following day, they know when to expect it and they want to know what all the fuss is about! It's important to offer maximum validity in terms of the dates that the Prospect can book but a limited booking window. As a general rule, you should allow Prospects to take advantage of the offer for up to six months, but it must be booked within the five-day sales window. Make sure the call-to-action is repeated no less than three times within the offer and where possible create multiple ways to book (call and online via a promotional code or promotional link). The repetition of the call-to-action is a crucial part of the process given that most email recipients tend to skim read and we want there to be zero ambiguity about what we want them to do next.

The use of telephone tracking numbers can be really useful here. Our preferred supplier Invoco provides local numbers all over the UK for a line rental of £1 per month. These numbers can be instantly redirected to your main reception line and the caller, not the receiver, knows no different.

> For more information on Invoco's services visit
> www.dhm.agency/suppliers

Firstly, the key benefit of telephone tracking is that you will be able to track the success of your email campaign by identifying how many times it prompted the phone to ring. Secondly, you will be able to see how many calls went unanswered, giving you and your team the opportunity to return these calls so you don't miss out on an opportunity to close a direct booking!

Send a follow-up email two days later informing your Prospects that the offer must end the next day at 5pm. You may also decide to broadcast an email the next day, two hours before the closing deadline, prompting any last-minute action.

Whilst this may feel a bit overkill to send this volume of emails in such a short window, our experience consistently shows that the follow up emails always outperform the first offer launch email. That is to say that more sales are received after Prospects have been reminded a second or third time than launching them the offer on the first attempt, despite all of the anticipation building put in place with the tease email. The final step is to officially shut the offer down when you said you would. Be clear about when the cut-off point is and make it very specific (5pm Tuesday for example). In order to create a successful buying environment, there must be a strict deadline.

Multi-Channel Marketing

Adopting the aforementioned sales campaign to make up the '6' days of the 55/6 rule can have a dramatic impact on your ability to command income at will from a group of well nurtured Prospects without having to sacrifice vast amounts of your profit to commission. But we don't want to stop there. These six days of selling are very important to your business and we want to ensure that every Prospect that knows, likes and trusts your business has the opportunity to take advantage of the high value offers you are making available within this buying environment window. To that end, we use something which I've come to term 'Facebook Ad Amplification'.

As the name suggests, we want to amplify your sales message across Facebook to ensure we spread the message as far and as wide as possible, but also because multi-channel marketing is exponentially more effective at cutting through the onslaught of marketing messages we as consumers are subjected to every day. If you see the same marketing message in more than one place it becomes harder to ignore. Be it a new car that you like the look of, a new series on Netflix that you're interested in or a brand of clothing you aspire to wear – those marketing messages are going to resonate and become more apparent if you see them advertised on Facebook, on the side of a bus and marketed to you directly by landing in your inbox.

Now, whilst I'm not advocating your hotel spending thousands on expensive ad campaigns, Facebook Ad Amplification is a low-cost way of using multi-channel marketing to your advantage.

Unbeknown to most hoteliers (and most marketers) Facebook allows you to upload your entire email database into its advertising platform. The reason you would choose to do this is to understand how many of your email addresses are associated with a Facebook account. Typically, you can find that anywhere between 40% and 60% of your database have also used the email you have on record to set up their Facebook account. You won't see who these Prospects are, but that's not important. The key here is that you can now advertise to a selection of your email recipients on Facebook encouraging them to check their inbox for the limited-time special offer exclusively available to them right now.

A 'Did you see the email?' and can be amazingly effective at encouraging Prospects to revert to their inboxes and revisit the emails that were overlooked the first time they scanned their inbox for anything worth reading. Dependent on the size of your audience, a small investment of £20-40 is normally sufficient.

> Take our online assessment now to understand how your hotel rates on our hotel marketing scale. Visit www.thedirectmethod.com

Part Two

The Browser Method

Chapter 7

The Browser Method: Introduction

Unlike a Prospect who already knows, likes and trusts your hotel – someone who isn't necessarily looking for a hotel stay but with the right offer communicated within the right buying environment may look to book – a browser doesn't yet know much about you.

A browser is someone who is actively looking for a hotel break. They're looking on Google, TripAdvisor, Trivago, Booking.com and all manner of other sites to find the right hotel at the right price, possibly for a special occasion of some sort. They probably know the specific dates they wish to stay, they know the broad location they wish to visit and have a budget in mind.

Browsers will often start their booking decision process on Google, typing in search terms such as 'Spa hotels in the Cotswolds' or something similar. They'll then almost always end up on a meta-search website like Trivago or an OTA like Booking.com. They'll start to get a feel for the prices and types of hotels on offer. They may even go to a review website like TripAdvisor to assist their decision-making process. At some point during this browsing process, they'll start to shortlist a few hotels that meet their booking criteria and come within budget. At this point all research points to the fact that most leisure bookers will head over to the websites of the hotels that they have shortlisted. This is likely to be the first time the browser has come into contact with your hotel outside of the big global travel agents and other travel websites.

Browsers of this nature don't need a buying environment like Prospects do; they already have enough impetus to book, they're just not sure yet if your hotel is the right one for them, nor if booking direct is the most convenient or highest value option for them. To put it another way, browsers need to be convinced and that will require all five aspects of The Browser Method impressive content, remarketing, social proof, a smooth browsing experience and to feel that their chosen booking method offers the highest perceived value.

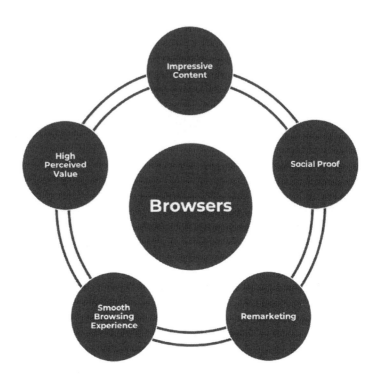

Organic vs Paid-For Browsers

The above description of the booking journey describes an organic browser: that is someone who has naturally come to your website having identified from other means that you are one of the hotels they are considering for their specific stay. A 'paid-for' browser is someone you have coerced to your website using a pay-per-click (PPC) advertising method. The most common of these would be Google AdWords, targeting ads to specific keywords relating to your product, e.g. hotels in London.

Despite PPC advertising on platforms like Google being something the DHM team have won awards for, and it's one of the things we're best known for, I'm only ever an advocate of PPC advertising for hotels as the very last thing within the marketing mix being used to get more direct bookings.

The reason for this is twofold:

1. Most independent hotel websites receive on average 5,000 unique users per month with approximately a 1% conversion rate, i.e. 50 bookings per month. That leaves 4,950 browsers that aren't booking or using an OTA to book. Whilst not all of these 4,950 browsers will have the intent, the means and the inclination to book your hotel, my argument is always that it makes more sense to try to convert a few more of the 4,950 that don't book each month than spending vast sums to acquire more traffic.

2. Secondly, most browsers start their booking-decision process on a search engine like Google and can take weeks or even months to make up their mind. You could end up paying £2 to get a click to your website on day one at the very start of a 60-day decision-making process. Whilst this isn't necessarily a bad idea per se, in most cases my advice is to let the deep pockets of the likes of Booking.com incur the cost on Google and let

the traffic come to you organically through these means.

To put it another way, why spend a great deal of time and effort trying to pick the highest apples off the tree when there are perfectly good apples landing at your feet? Second to Prospects, organic browsers are your next lowest hanging fruit.

What's Important to a Browser?

Naturally, it depends on the purpose of their stay. A couple that are visiting a specific area to attend a family wedding will be looking for a night's accommodation within close proximity to the wedding venue. Location is likely to be one of the most important factors in this case. Comparatively, an individual looking to surprise their partner with an anniversary break may prioritise the hotel's facilities amongst all other things. If he/she believes having a spa and a four-poster bed with a roll-top bath in the corner of the room is of most importance, they may equally consider a hotel 100 miles north and 100 miles south of their own location.

Irrespective of the individual browser's priorities and motivations for their hotel booking, as hoteliers it's your job to communicate the core selling points of the property in the best possible way, and to lean your communications towards the frequent reasons your hotel is chosen amongst all others so that you maximise bookings. The Browser Method will show you the formula within which these communications can be best used to encourage more direct bookings.

Take our online assessment now to understand how your hotel rates on our hotel marketing scale. Visit www.thedirectmethod.com

Chapter 8

The Browser Method: Impressive Content

Forgive the obvious nature of this point but great photography is an absolute must for every hotel. Despite being obvious, it needs to be explored because at DHM there has been countless conversations with clients about what constitutes great photography – and all too often when we ask for images to be sent across for us to work with, the quality is substandard.

What I mean by this is, often a professional photographer has not taken them, so the images are low-resolution and pixelated, taken on a phone, have poor lighting, depict bedroom images with creased bed linen, or my absolute bug-bear, taken portrait not landscape. A portrait image has almost zero purpose when it comes to digital marketing.

The problem here is that imagery can look stunning or look amateur and it carries so much influence on booking decisions. The adage that a picture is worth a thousand words holds true and I would even take it further to say that a stunning hotel image is worth a thousand bookings. And yet I'm labouring the point here because over the years I have seen hoteliers spend £500,000 on a refurbishment project to then use shots taken on an iPhone to sell it!

Now smart phone cameras may have come a long way and I'm sure someone who knows their camera specs will tell you that the number of megapixels in the average mobile phone camera is more than sufficient to produce the resolution needed – but as with everything, the right tools in the wrong hands won't produce the desired result.

Photography is an art form that is studied for years by professionals and to ensure you are doing your product justice, it deserves a professional to bring it to life through stunning imagery. That said, authenticity is key. There's really no point conveying luxury within a 2-star property nor should you show only the refurbished rooms when the non-refurbished rooms will serve to disappoint the guest. A balance is critical, and a great professional photographer can do that.

Browsers Need Great Photography

The average browser that lands on your website is likely to have found your business on a much bigger travel agent, meta-search site or indeed a review website, so it's important to have consistency across the board when it comes to your imagery. Whilst the subject of this book is undeniably about increasing direct bookings, OTAs like Booking.com still have a significant role to play in encouraging those bookings direct.

As such it's important to ensure your imagery is high quality on your Booking.com page. As discussed in the previous chapter, it is common for a browser to start their search on Google, head to Booking.com, find a few hotels that match the browser's criteria and budget and then head over to the individual hotel's website.

As you'll no doubt be aware, images can be uploaded very easily within the Booking.com extranet. By taking a scroll through a series of hotel pages on Booking.com you'll be met by a multitude of images that are low resolution, the wrong size or worse, the orientation of the image is portrait. Give your hotel the best possible chance by ensuring your imagery on this channel and other OTAs is as best as it can possibly look.

The other area that is often overlooked is the Google Knowledge Panel. This is the box on the right-hand side of Google when a specific business is typed in on a desktop or tablet. If you punch in your own hotel's name you should see this box with a series of images (inside and out) a map of the location and some key information about the property such as address and opening hours. This information is completely editable using the Google My Business tool. If no one within your hotel has ever edited this content, Google will probably have guessed (pretty accurately) at this information. What it's not quite so good at is choosing the best imagery for your business. By gaining access to your Google Knowledge Panel you can edit these images to ensure your hotel is looking its best when a browser comes knocking.

When a browser finally makes it over to your website, imagery is one of the first things that determine whether they wish to explore further. This is where the website's bounce rate is important. A 'bounce' on a website happens when a browser lands on your site, does nothing and leaves. In the event of this happening they may have got distracted (some do) but a high bounce rate is often an indication that the browser has not been impressed with the look of the website or probably the image that greeted them on the page loading. One of the reasons can be imagery that is not appropriate for the current season. Being greeted with an image depicting a beautiful summer's day with Pimm's on the lawn outside the hotel in the depths of winter probably isn't all that congruent with the browser's expectations at that time of year.

Equally, arriving at a website that's promoting the Valentine's Day dinner menu in April instantly gives the wrong impression to the browser and can impact the bounce rate. This is explored in more detail in the Smooth Browsing Experience chapter.

Videography

At the time of writing (April 2018), video is going through a huge period of accelerated growth. If you use Facebook in your personal life or for your own hotel, you will have noticed a great deal more video in your newsfeed. YouTube is now the second largest search engine on the planet and the emergence of Facebook Live recently has proliferated this trend too.

What this means for your hotel is that now is more important than ever to be bringing your product to life through video. What this doesn't mean, however, is to spend a fortune to create one stunning 10-minute video that all-encompasses your hotel. Rather you need lots of different videos all timed somewhere from 30-75 seconds. The reason for this is that people's attention spans have become reduced significantly. When you consider a platform like Facebook, you're only a short finger movement away from the next video or post. In the same way that a newspaper article always seems to look more interesting over the shoulder of your partner or someone you're sitting next to on a train, the next video might, just might, be a little more interesting.

When it comes to Facebook, video also offers some reach benefits. In general terms, your Facebook post will achieve a higher organic reach if you were to post video, rather than a single image, series of images or a text post. This is mainly because Facebook knows that video is a better way to engage with its users and it wants them to stay on Facebook for longer. Why? Well if you stay on Facebook for longer, you are more likely to engage with sponsored posts which means Facebook makes more money. No surprise there!

Your videos should also sit on your website. Browsers who are considering staying at your hotel want to see what your property is like and nothing does this better than video. A common website trend in recent years has seen a full-bleed (no borders), sound-free video embedded into the background of the site that starts on auto-play when a user lands on the website. In a hotel where no two rooms are the same we often advise the creation of a 40-second video for each room – this might feel a bit overkill but when you consider that a browser is about to spend several hundred pounds on a room for the weekend, and it's for an important special occasion like a birthday, anniversary or even an engagement, then it makes sense to communicate to this potential customer exactly what they can expect from their stay. Moreover, most hotels don't do this, so it can give your property a distinct advantage over your nearest competition.

Three Types of Video You Need

There are three types of video you need to convince your browsers that your hotel is the best possible choice.

1. Product Videos

    These are videos that showcase the hotel and bring it to life in the browsers mind. You'll naturally want to show individual rooms or at the very least, room types, with a music bed appropriate to the style and character of your property. Communal areas like reception, lounge, restaurant and patio are important to convey. A good videographer can capture these in ways you perhaps have not imagined before. Drone shots that give an aerial view of the property can also be great at showing the grandeur or stunning location of the hotel.

2. Team Interviews

Interview videos with staff members or the management/ownership team is something that you don't see enough. Yet, at its very heart, hotels are people businesses. Long after a guest forgets the décor, they'll still remember the waiter that went the extra mile. Service is everything in hotels and it's the people that deliver the service so including them in the browser's consideration process is key. Having the owner or the general manager sitting in front of a beautiful backdrop, explaining his/her passion and vision for the hotel, what they want the guest to experience and even their own personal philosophy of what a superb hotel stay should be can be so powerful for the browser.

This process shouldn't stop at the management. Having your head chef explaining what the menu is all about or why the waiting staff love working at your hotel or even having the night porter sharing some stories of bizarre requests they've received in their time in the job can ooze personality and leave a lasting impression on the browser.

The style and type of hotel you have will determine whether the video personality should be tongue-in-cheek or prim and proper.

Regardless of whether you run a quirky boutique or a traditional country house hotel, having your people featured in video in the right ways will lift you head and shoulders above your competition in the browser's mind.

3. Customer Testimonials

Again, these videos are rare for hotels. This type of video is discussed more within the Social Proof chapter.

Chapter 9

The Browser Method: Social Proof

The Importance of Reviews

We all know that in recent years, the emergence of review websites like TripAdvisor have impacted the way in which consumers book hotels and current research points to the fact that the influence of these review websites is growing. The challenge hotcliers face is that online reviews have made the consumer question their hotel choice. It is not uncommon for a browser to find a hotel that matches their booking criteria and come within their budget, only to see a handful of 1-star TripAdvisor reviews or a 7.6 review score on a site like Booking.com or Trivago and begin to question their decision, choosing instead to continue their research rather than acting at that moment.

Just as likely, however, is the use of review websites or social proof to validate a booking decision. If a browser is 95% certain that a hotel is the one for them, they may see a plethora of rave reviews and feel that their choice is validated, which in turn gives them the impetus and confidence to book.

Very often browsers will also use reviews to steer their research rather than to use them to question or validate. In this case, a browser may start their booking process on a site like TripAdvisor and search for the top hotels in a given location and work their way from there.

Irrespective of the role that social proof plays in the browser's booking decision, it is irrefutable that good reviews help to win business and bad reviews can cost your business. To that end, regardless of your own personal view of sites like TripAdvisor, it's more important than ever to encourage positive feedback about your hotel and the best hotels don't leave this to chance.

Review Filter

Many years ago, I visited a friend who at the time owned a hotel on the south coast of England. He introduced me to a piece of software he developed that 'keeps the bad reviews off TripAdvisor'. Naturally I was intrigued to learn more and since that day we at DHM have implemented this tool in almost every hotel we have worked with to great effect. Unlike many reputation management solutions, Review Filter has no affiliation nor a relationship with TripAdvisor. It was developed by a hotelier, for hoteliers and its core objective (as the name suggests) is to filter bad reviews so that they are kept behind closed doors, so to speak, and away from the eyes of potential customers.

Here's how it works: within a few hours of check-out an email is sent automatically to the guest thanking them for their custom and asking them to click on a link to leave a review. Most property management systems (PMS) do something similar, but the difference that Review Filter offers is that it sends the guest to a special page where they can leave a one- to five-star rating, a personal review and click the submit button.

Cleverly, if the review is rated one, two or three stars, three things happen when the 'submit' button is pressed. The first is that a real-time automated message is sent to an email address of your choosing (be it Front of House Manager, General Manager etc.) informing the hotel of who the guest is, their contact information and the negative review that the guest has just left. Should you wish to contact the guest to discuss and resolve the issues that have prompted this negative review is entirely up to the hotel but it's something we advise in most instances.

The second thing that happens is the guest is taken to a page that apologises that their expectations haven't been met and that someone from the hotel will be in touch shortly to discuss their poor experience. The third and probably most significant aspect is that the negative review is lost forever for the guest. Even if they press the backspace button they will be met with a blank screen. This is important because the last thing we want the guest to do is press submit, backtrack to the previous page so they can copy their review, then head over to TripAdvisor and paste in their review. The negative review in this instance of course is only available for the hotel to see and action, allowing them to receive the feedback without it being banded across the Internet for all to see. This method works because it gives a disgruntled guest the space to vent their frustration without it damaging the hotel's online reputation.

Contrastingly, if the review received on that first page has been rated four- or five-stars, when the guest clicks on the submit button, they are taken to a completely different page. On this new page the happy guest will find a two-click process with which they are invited and encouraged to follow which leads them conveniently to the TripAdvisor review submission page of the hotel.

In summary, the tool exists to push good reviews to sites like TripAdvisor and makes it difficult for bad reviews to go beyond the hotel so they can be handled and dealt with behind closed doors. To put it another way, it's the digital equivalent of your receptionist checking guests out with a stack of TripAdvisor cards in their pocket, asking each guest how their experience was. If they respond positively, that receptionist will probably take a card out and ask if they would kindly write something about their experience on TripAdvisor. Equally, if the guest is somewhat disappointed with their experience you can be sure that TripAdvisor card is going nowhere near that guest. Review Filter acts in exactly the same way.

Over the years of presenting this solution to hoteliers all over the world, I'm often met with some scepticism about how ethical this process is given that you are influencing (or some might argue manipulating) what browsers see. My viewpoint on this is very firm: these guests are YOUR customers – you can ask for feedback any which way you choose – Review Filter simply provides a channel for your hotel to obtain real time feedback on a guest's experience and encourages the nice things to be posted online and discourages the bad things from ever being seen.

Let it be known, however, that whilst this tool is effective it can't control your TripAdvisor page or any other review site for that matter. If you worry that using a tool like Review Filter will simply have your TripAdvisor page awash with five-star reviews giving it an unauthentic look, it just won't happen. The occasional bad reviews will still find their way onto these sites, but it helps to have a little influence rather than leaving it all to chance.

For more information on how Review Filter works visit www.dhm.agency/suppliers

Video Testimonials

Arguably, more influential than written reviews are video testimonials. At the Cranleigh Boutique we've used these to great effect, capturing on camera delighted guests who are positively beaming about their experience with the hotel. This form of video is probably the most underused within the industry, yet happy customer videos are seen in almost all other walks of business and life.

Imagine that a 40-year-old female is scrolling through your hotel's website looking for the right hotel to celebrate her wedding anniversary, and she stumbles across another 40-something couple that also visited this particular hotel for their anniversary. On this video the pair explain how they were overwhelmed at the care and attention to detail the hotel offered and how their anniversary was made really special as a result. Finding customers who are well suited to your typical demographic who are happy to share their experience with passion on camera in an articulate and authentic way can carry so much influence for that browser who is currently weighing up their options.

Chapter 10

The Browser Method: Remarketing

Remarketing was covered at length in Chapter 5 and remarketing with the intention of targeting browsers is not a great deal different to remarketing to Prospects. However, when you consider that the average customer doesn't know how remarketing advertising works – that it's based on a pay-per-click basis not a pay-per-impressions basis – this can be used to your advantage. The typical browser can spend hours of research time that can often span weeks or even months before choosing the hotel that's right for them. In this time, they may see your ads on some of the biggest websites on the Internet such as mailonline.com, cnn.com or goodhousekeeping.co.uk or wherever they happen to be browsing). Having a presence on these websites can give your hotel the gravitas of being associated with these global brands, even if it is in the form of advertising space.

Arguably though, the core benefit within the context of browsers is that most hotels which are within the browser's shortlist almost certainly won't be using remarketing advertising to their advantage. In the 500+ hotels I've met with since DHM was started in 2012, I can count on one hand the number of hotels that use, or have even heard of, remarketing as a means of advertising their business.

Let's also not forget that the Direct Method is about encouraging those bookings to come to you via the telephone or through your own website, and not through a third party. If a browser has visited your hotel's page on Booking.com before they visited your website, then chances are that Booking.com will be remarketing your hotel back to the browser, possibly also advertising a 'from rate' to entice the browser back to complete their booking.

What we want to ensure is that your remarketing advertising is very clearly communicating the benefits of booking direct within these ads. Whether those reasons are price-led (e.g. book direct for best price) or value-led (tangible benefits like late check-out or free drink for booking direct) the reasons for booking direct must be clear and concise.

Dynamic Remarketing

The aforementioned example from Booking.com advertising your own hotel back to the browser is a form of advanced advertising called dynamic remarketing when advertising through Google AdWords. The idea is that rather than Booking.com advertising themselves, they are advertising the exact hotel and, in some cases, the exact room types or even the rates for the specific nights the browser had previously searched. The more specific you can be with your remarketing the better as this level of detail will resonate more clearly than simply the name of the hotel. The slight drawback with this form of advertising, however, is that you usually need large volumes of traffic for it to be effective. To that end, for most hotels a standard remarketing campaign will be sufficient.

Chapter 11

The Browser Method: Smooth Browsing Experience

What the OTAs are undeniably great at is creating a smooth browsing experience. Booking.com in particular make the process pretty hurdle-free and seamless in helping you navigate across millions of hotels available on their complex database of inventory.

Comparatively, what independent hotels are notoriously bad at is making the booking process clunky, complex and outright difficult to make a booking through their website. The challenge, of course, is that even if your website is offering a lower price, you're still battling against a world-class booking functionality that offers a slick and convenient solution to making a booking online. And inevitably, in lots of cases, having a booking functionality that rivals the global brands doesn't often come cheap.

The frustration, of course, is that if a smooth browsing experience isn't invested in, as a hotel you'll end up paying in other ways. At best in the form of commission; at worst by missing out on the business to a competitor.

Inevitably, like with most things in life, let alone marketing, getting to the exact formula on what constitutes a smooth browsing experience takes time – there's no quick fix. Spending a hefty sum on a brand new website and feeling that it 'sells you well' and is easy to navigate almost always means that money is being left on the table. We've seen beautiful websites that make the hotel look stunning that convert less than 0.2% of traffic, or clever menu bars that the hoteliers love for its simplicity that end up causing a bounce rate of over 50% because browsers don't immediately know how to navigate the site and choose to leave before spending the extra few seconds required to work it out. We refer to this as 'browser friction'. If you create too much friction for the browser during their experience with your website, they'll get fed up and leave. Sometimes the issues are obvious and with a couple of tweaks here and there the performance of the website can improve dramatically. Often, though, a great deal of tweaking, coupled with careful measurement is needed to understand how to improve conversion. In short, building a stunning website is just the start; making it convert at its optimum point takes time, patience and a lot of know-how.

Conversion Rate Optimisation

If you're not familiar with this term, you're not alone. Approximately 5% of hoteliers I've come into contact with in the last few years are familiar with this, and probably only about 70% of marketers. That's not to suggest that it's a particularly new discipline, far from it, but it's scarcely used across the hotel industry in my experience. If you consider that the objective of Search Engine Optimisation (SEO) is to get your website to rank higher on search engines like Google and Bing, thus delivering your website more organic traffic, the objective of Conversion Rate Optimisation (CRO) is to have your website convert more of that traffic into bookers. To put it another way, imagine that your website is a bucket with lots of little holes in the bottom. These holes represent where people are having trouble navigating your website and leaving. In most cases, there are so many holes that 99% of the water you put into that bucket goes straight through them. In an attempt to get more water to stay into the bucket you have two options:

a. Try putting more water into the bucket (SEO)

b. Try to plug some of these holes (CRO)

In this analogy it would be a foolish waste of time and money putting more water into the bucket without first attempting to find ways to make those holes smaller. And yet often the first port of call for any business who wants more bookings coming through their website is to add more traffic.

Consider a website with 5,000 unique users per month and a conversion rate percentage of 1% – they would get 50 bookings per month through their website. Now if this hotel wanted to work towards doubling their bookings to 100 per month, they really have two main options:

a. Find ways to double the traffic to 10,000 unique users per month

b. Try to double the conversion rate from 1% to 2%

It should go without saying which of these two options would be easier and cheaper. The latter, by the way, would only mean finding an additional 50 bookings from the 4,950 that visited but didn't book. The former requires finding an additional 5,000 visitors to the website!

When you start to focus on conversion as a meaningful metric, it can steer your decision making when it comes to understanding whether your hotel should be spending on pay-per-click (PPC) advertising or Search Engine Optimisation (SEO). Logic dictates that investing in improving the performance of your website's conversion would be a better first step than investing in more traffic to your website.

When it comes to CRO, we care about three metrics:

a. Bounce rate

b. Website conversion percentage

c. Telephone conversion percentage

When applying our CRO strategy at DHM, our aim is to reduce the bounce rate of the website and improve the website and telephone conversion percentages.

To clarify these terms: the 'bounce rate' of a website is the percentage of users that arrive on a website, do nothing and leave. The 'website conversion percentage' is the number of unique users that go on to make a booking. The 'telephone conversion percentage' is the number of unique users that call the hotel to make a booking. The last metric can be difficult to track as these bookings could have been taken by 10 different staff members over a month-long period so as a general rule we make an estimate by tracking the number of calls that came from the website that lasted two minutes or longer. We're able to track this by using a unique tracking number which would typically have a local area code which simply and easily redirects to the main line of the hotel.

This probably reads very logically but you might be thinking, 'How does it all work?' Well the digital world offers all manner of tools to help you draw insights that might lead to a better conversion rate. Google Analytics is a free tool that allows you to understand not just how much traffic your website gets, but also where that traffic is leaving your website. It can tell you that 20% of your traffic leaves the website on the image gallery page, for example, or that since you installed that homepage slider of images, the bounce rate has increased by 15%. These are helpful insights that can help you 'plug some of the holes' that are causing you to lose browsers from your website who may otherwise have booked.

There are also more advanced tools that allow you to view heat-maps of your web pages so you can see where the biggest concentration of clicks have been. Moving your desired call-to-action (e.g. 'Book Now' button) into those areas with the largest concentration of mouse movement may increase your calls-to-action by a few percentage points. You can even use software to 'spy' on your website browsers. It will record the browsers' interaction with your website, so you can start to draw insight from them. Having watched anywhere between 10 and 100 screen videos (not the most riveting of exercises I can assure you!) you may be able to see that 80% of your sample scroll down, scroll back up and click on the 'Image Gallery' tab in the menu bar – which may prompt you to make the availability checking widget much more prominent on the image gallery.

Understanding Benchmark Figures

Measuring these metrics and drawing insight so that they can be improved upon is all well and good but to determine whether a real increase in bookings is happening, it's important to understand the benchmark figures. These figures ideally need to be monthly as many hotels tend to be seasonal which can ultimately impact the conversion figures. Typically, to understand the monthly benchmark website conversion figures for the year we would take the conversion figures from the last two years for the month of January, then work out the average.

For example:

	Website Traffic	No. Bookings	Conversion Rate
January 2016	4,784	38	0.79%
January 2017	4,679	41	0.88%
		AVERAGE:	**0.84%**

In this example the average (or benchmark) website conversion rate for the month of January is 0.84%. When we come to record the website conversion percentage, anything above 0.84% is considered an uplift.

For example:

	Website Traffic	No. Bookings	Conversion Rate
January 2018	4,612	47	1.02%
		UPLIFT:	**+0.18%**

Similarly, we find benchmark figures for the bounce rate and the telephone conversion percentage. The latter tends not to have historical data so ordinarily you'd look to work with 2-3 months of data before making any amendments to the website.

The 12 Steps to Better Conversion

Over the years at DHM, having improved the conversion of dozens of hotel websites, we've created a framework that can help us to work faster. These 12 steps are by no means a one-size-fits-all given each hotel is unique and certainly doesn't negate the need for studying each individual website's data to find valuable insights that can steer the conversion in the right ways. That said they offer a helpful checklist:

1. Social media icons

   All too often you arrive on a hotel's website with a selection of social media icons in the top navigation. This is a mistake that can inhibit the conversion rate. When you think about it, it doesn't make a great deal of sense to drive your browsers away from your website and onto a social platform offering a never-ending supply of distractions. If you're driving people to Facebook, an old school friend could start communicating with your browser via the Messenger function. If it's Instagram they could have a notification that a few more likes have been received from their post earlier in the day which takes their attention away from your hotel and back on that selfie they posted three hours earlier! The key is that social channels should exist to drive traffic *to* your website, not from it. Moving those social media icons to the footer or off the website completely can help keep browsers on your website for longer.

2. Availability checker above the fold

   The term 'above the fold' is most commonly associated with broadsheet newspapers where there is a literal fold in the newspaper. Websites bizarrely have adopted the same term referring to the area of the website that is viewed upon the homepage loading on a desktop or tablet. Whilst it might seem trivial, having the availability checker widget 'above the fold' can have a significant improvement on the conversion of a website. All too often when browsing hotel websites, actually finding the area where you can check if your desired dates are available can prove challenging. This can cause unnecessary browser friction.

3. Location and Positioning Statement above the fold

It is often taken for granted that your browsers will know the general location of your hotel when they arrive on your website but it's not always the case. A browser who has a main booking criterion of finding a hotel with spa facilities within 2-3 hours from London, could just as well be looking in the Cotswolds, Peak District and the South Downs for their hotel – all of which are several hundred miles from one another. As such in this instance, the browser may land on your website and can't quite remember whereabouts the hotel is located, prompting them to search through the menu bar for the contact page just so they can see your address. Rather than listing your address on the header or menu bar, a positioning statement that includes your location can be a useful tool to reduce the bounce rate. A positioning statement is simply a few words that summarise your hotel in the browsers mind when they have landed on your hotel for the first time.

Some examples:

'The Peak District's most dog-friendly hotel'

'Stunning spa hotel in the heart of the Lake District'

'Luxury country escape 30 miles from London'

'Norfolk's premier wedding venue'

What to include within a positioning statement will largely depend on the type of hotel you have and the typical clientele you serve. It's worth spending some time to understand what positioning statement could work best for you as these few short words as listed above can instantly summarise your property in the browser's mind so they don't have to spend time working it out for themselves.

4. Website copy

Copy-writing is one of those things that anyone can do, but only a few people can do well. Getting the copy right on your website so that it conveys the hotel's style and character can be challenging but very rewarding. A quirky, characterful boutique could be a little tongue-in-cheek with their language whereas a more traditional regal property would want to maintain a level of formality in its style.

5. Multiple language add-on/plug-ins

    It goes without saying that if your hotel welcomes guests from overseas, having a multi-language plug-in can help to improve conversion from these types of customers. Depending on how your website has been built, this can be both incredibly cheap and fast to implement or expensive and slow. Key markets may be China, Japan, Germany, France or Spain; having your website quickly and easily accessible to browsers in their native language will almost certainly improve conversion if you are receiving considerable traffic from browsers in these countries.

6. Hero image change

    The 'hero' image is normally the first image the browser sees when they land on your website. It is often an exterior shot and is the image that you feel provides an all-encompassing overview of your hotel. Within the CRO strategy we like to play around with this, changing it up regularly as often the hero image can influence the bounce rate of the website. Using a drone shot instead of a ground shot could halve the bounce rate, for example.

7. Tweaking the 'Book Now' button

    Whilst this also might seem like a trivial change, the colour and the prominence of the 'Book Now' button can help to encourage more browsers to move onto the booking pages. There's no set rule as each hotel and its respective browsers are different but testing and measuring these over several months can give you incremental, albeit marginal, gains that work towards improving the overall conversion. What can be particularly useful is viewing a heat-map of your homepage to understand where the highest concentration of mouse movement is, then moving the 'Book Now' button to that area. Similarly effective could be changing the words from 'Book Now' to 'Check Availability' – albeit a subtle change, this may improve results given that some browsers may feel a sense of finality about seeing the words 'Book Now' when actually they're not quite sure if they're ready to commit to their booking but may well be happy to commit to checking availability.

8. <u>Messenger Bot</u>

An online chat facility is nothing new, they've been around for some time but what has recently come onto the mainstream market are messenger bots. Working in very much the same way as an online messenger service, they use a form of artificial intelligence to interact with the browser, answer any basic questions that they may have and pass the enquiry onto a real person who can engage the browser at the hotel. This can be a really useful tool given that as far as the browser is concerned, they are having a conversation with a real person. There are downsides, of course, and it should go without saying that some browsers may find this annoying which is the very opposite of what we're trying to do for their browsing experience. As with every one of these, it's important to test and measure.

9. <u>Pop-Up</u>

A pop-up on the website offering a special discount code for booking direct or promoting the advantages of booking direct can be very useful at encouraging the browser to engage further with the website. Just as likely it can cause browser friction and become annoying. When adopting a pop-up as part of the CRO strategy, there's a fine balance here and ultimately what matters most is whether the three-core metrics move in the intended direction. This one's not for every hotel.

10. Sticky Menu Bar

The menu bar that typically contains your website's top-navigation should be present at all times. We refer to this as 'sticky' so regardless of where the user happens to be browsing on the website the menu bar sticks to the top of the page. It's advisable to keep the telephone number, 'Book Now' button/availability checker widget and the website's main navigation viewable at all times. You never know when each individual browser will have seen enough to feel that you're the right hotel for them and the last thing we would want to do is cause unnecessary browser friction at the point where they are likely to move closer to booking.

11. Auto-play video background or sliders

Reducing the bounce rate is an important part of the CRO process and much of it depends on what the browser sees and experiences within the first 5-7 seconds of landing on the website. As mentioned previously, an auto-play video background can work nicely to instantly give the browser an understanding of what the hotel's key selling points are. Equally an image slider (sometimes called a carousel) can do this too. The challenge is that you really have no idea until you try it. Finding the optimum initial visual experience so that the bounce rate is reduced to its lowest possible point is a working process but certainly worth pursuing.

12. Notification pop-ups

A notification pop-up is less intrusive than a regular pop-up (also referred to as a modal lightbox) that takes up the whole webpage. The best examples of these can be seen on Booking.com in the form of a small box that appears in one of the corners of the screens informing you that 17 people are looking at this hotel right now or that 78 bookings have been made to this hotel in the last 48 hours. Armed with the right (authentic!) message, these can be a subtle way of providing a little social proof and urgency to encourage the browser to make their decision. Seeing that there are only two rooms available on the browser's desired dates and that there are 12 people looking at this hotel right now may be the gentle nudge needed to turn the browser into a booker.

Split-testing to Improve Conversion

These 12 steps offer a guide on how conversion can be increased on a website but if implemented in incorrect ways can have a detrimental effect. One way of reducing the risk if you're new to the world of CRO implementation is to use a tool like VWO (Visual Website Optimiser) which allows you to make subtle changes to your website and only have a percentage of your browsers view the amended version. For example, you may want to change the homepage image to a bedroom rather than the existing exterior shot but rather than risking a full month's traffic to see if the bounce rate is reduced, you feed 25% of the traffic to the bedroom image version and 75% of the traffic to the exterior shot version. At DHM it's common for our website suggestions to be met with hesitation and a healthy dose of scepticism by our clients – this percentage split-testing approach allows us to test our hypothesis with minimal risk and feedback our findings to the client.

Booking Engines

Gradually, month by month an upward trend should begin to appear on the two-conversion metrics (website and telephone calls over two minutes) and a downward trend should appear on the bounce rate. But (and this is a very big BUT) what has been explored so far is about creating a smooth browsing experience so that we encourage more browsers to click on the 'Book Now' button. This unfortunately is only half the battle. The browsing experience could be super-slick and effective at convincing the browser to book, only to then have the browser be greeted with a slow, confusing booking engine offering over 100 different rates showing dates that weren't originally searched for. Whilst this might sound an extreme example, this is exactly what the browser sees when a hotel uses the current booking function of one the UK's biggest PMS providers. The last thing we want is for all the hard work of getting the browser to the booking page to then paralyse them with choice causing more browser friction than at any other point during their browsing experience right when they were about to get out their credit card!

Having worked with every major PMS and booking engine, it's taken us a great deal of time at DHM to feel comfortable about recommending one to our clients but having now worked with Avvio and seen what it's capable of across a multitude of hotels, it's our preferred choice. At the time of writing, it's the only booking engine on the market that uses artificial intelligence to make the browsing experience smoother and they offer a guarantee that direct bookings will improve by 25% which speaks for itself as a selling point.

For more information about why we actively recommend Avvio visit
www.dhm.agency/suppliers

Chapter 12

High Perceived Value

Having created really impressive content and authentic social proof, as well as remarketed effectively and created a smooth browsing experience, The Browser Method will be largely ineffective if the browser does not perceive the rate for their chosen dates to be of high value. Inevitably savvy browsers will be asking themselves, if only subconsciously, 'Is this the best value hotel for my needs?' and 'If yes, is this the highest value rate for this hotel that I can find?'

It's not about being the Cheapest Hotel

The words 'high perceived value' have been chosen very carefully in this chapter and you'd be forgiven for thinking I'm suggesting being the cheapest hotel – for clarity's sake: that is NOT what I'm suggesting. For the browser, what constitutes 'high value' is all about their perception. In some cases, being £10 cheaper per night than your closest competitors still won't give your hotel the perception of higher value. Often what affects this perception is the reason the browser is booking. Now whilst all customers are different with different needs, they can be loosely pigeon-holed into distinct groups with similar needs.

Gaining a deep understanding of your customers' reasons for staying will help you to charge accordingly. The business traveller may choose your hotel over a branded alternative as you offer free internet and free parking, even though your hotel is £10 more expensive. The excited 20-something who wants to pop the question to his partner may want the most expensive suite in the location of choice because he may perceive that a higher price per night will ultimately give him the prestige and luxury he desires most from his stay. Perceived value could even be something a little more obscure; like a retired couple who are keen to find a hotel with a log fire in the communal lounge, despite there being many cheaper alternatives without the feature.

In short, this concept of 'value' is often nothing more than a perception in the browser's mind and if you have 'sold' your property well during the browsing experience, it will allow your hotel to price your rooms accordingly so that competing on price isn't the only strategy.

Communicating the Benefits of Booking Direct

So let's assume that you've successfully convinced the browser that your hotel is the right one for them – now they want to make sure that they are getting the best possible rate. With the wealth of booking options available to customers in recent years, there has been a huge influx of savviness from guests. No longer do the majority take a rate for granted as the only one; they understand more than ever that a little shopping around can shave a hefty chunk off the price. The super-savvy browsers will know the levels of commission hotels pay to the OTAs and deal websites and telephone the hotel direct to see if that rate can be bettered, though in my experience it is still relatively rare.

What happens all too often, however, especially with independent hotels, is that the rate parity can be all over the place. More times than I care to remember, my partner has been researching hotels for us to visit for a short break, only to find that the one she has chosen offers a cheaper rate through an OTA than available on the hotel's own website. It should go without saying that regardless of how effectively you adopt The Browser Method into your own hotel, if an OTA is offering your rooms at a cheaper rate you're fighting a losing battle.

The Direct Booking Challenge

The problem that all hoteliers face is that OTAs offer many things that an individual hotel can't, or otherwise don't.

1. <u>Convenience</u>

   The likes of Booking.com have made the booking process so easy and convenient. When you already have an account, you are only a handful of clicks away from securing your booking. Compare this to a hotel that you've never stayed at before where you have to input all of your information such as name, email, postal address, credit card information and even in some cases less memorable information such as passport number. Almost every time a browser will find it more convenient to book with an OTA.

2. <u>Rewards and Cashback</u>

   Whether it's the clever loyalty scheme from Hotels.com where the user is offered his/her tenth hotel stay free or cashback websites like TopCashback.co.uk where the user can claim up to 11% back on their stay just by clicking from one of these websites onto an OTA website, the incentives offered can be near impossible to compete with.

3. <u>Free Cancellation</u>

   Some years ago, the OTAs began offering 'free cancellation' for many hotels giving guests the chance to cancel as little as 24 hours before without fear of losing money. This useful booking option offers a hassle-free, commitment-free incentive for the guest to book, giving them peace of mind that they can walk away should their plans change.

4. Security

There can at times be the concern that customers will be inputting their credit card information into a hotel's website that may not be secure. At the extreme end, the hotel doesn't actually exist and it's a complete scam or more likely that a poorly paid receptionist will steal their credit card information or their identity. The concern can be greater for international guests so booking through a trusted global OTA can overcome this issue.

5. Secret Discounts

The likes of the Booking.com 'Genius' discount offers regular bookers an additional 10% off the rates advertised which can be a nice incentive for the guest to book through this channel and a difficult aspect to manage across the hotel's own website to ensure they are priced competitively.

There may well be other reasons for choosing an OTA rather than booking direct for each individual browser, making it ever more challenging to secure the booking direct. But all is not lost!

By communicating the benefits of booking direct throughout the browsing experience, you can encourage guests to book through your website or over the telephone not just by offering a more desirable rate, but by offering more value.

At the time of writing, rate parity is a contentious issue in the hotel industry with many OTAs threatening to reduce your hotel's visibility (or remove completely in some cases) on their websites if your rates are seen to be offered lower on your own website. Whilst it would be wrong to advise you to ignore the threats from these OTAs, often a clever way around this is to offer more value.

Many of the hotels we work with at DHM offer things like free breakfast, free parking, free Internet and late check-out on their own website which represents significantly more value than the alternative offered through OTA sites. Finding ways to communicate the additional benefits of booking direct and having your website rates priced in a favourable way goes beyond the scope of this book and is typically part of a much wider revenue management strategy.

> For more information about DHM's revenue management services visit
> www.dhm.agency/revenue

Part Three

The Wedding Method

Chapter 13

The Wedding Method: Introduction

The Challenge of Securing Wedding Business

In recent years, there has been a vast proliferation of wedding venues entering the market. Keen to snap up a slice of the lucrative section of hospitality, more hoteliers and venue owners have started to position their business as a destination wedding venue, many with the aim of reaching 50+ weddings per year. In the ten years I've been involved in hotel marketing, there has been a great deal more 'converted barn' venues entering the wedding market. This, of course, isn't necessarily a bad thing for consumers but for the hoteliers who rely on a healthy batch of weddings on their books each year, it has become harder to secure the same volume of weddings they were achieving five or ten years ago. In many sought-after geographical areas, the wedding market has become so saturated that you could have 20 wedding venues in the same two-mile radius.

Yet, arguably, there should be more weddings to go around given that same-sex marriages have become commonplace and there has been a proliferation of second (or even third) weddings from the 40+ market in recent years.

Not only has the choice increased for engaged couples, the accessibility to this wider choice of venues has become greater too. Where only ten years ago a bride-to-be would mostly have looked to glossy wedding magazines for inspiration, now Facebook, Pinterest and Instagram are the first port of call for many. These social media websites offer a wider choice of venues and ideas given hotels need little more than an image and a few hashtags to get noticed. Also prominent will be websites like Hitched – a one-stop shop for engaged couples to browse all the options available to them on one convenient website.

Added to this challenge is that, across the board, couples are tending to spend less (and often expect more) on their big day. This is, of course, a sweeping generalisation but in our experience most hotels we work with used to average £4,000-£5,000 more per wedding than in recent years.

In today's British market, it is the norm for an engaged couple to subscribe to a couple of dozen different wedding venues and enquire about their packages. Across these 20-30 venues they could include grand castle hotels, small country house hotels and even French chateaux and Spanish villas. Having your venue (which almost always isn't the most spectacular in the enquiry list) stand out in such a crowded and noisy market place can be really challenging.

The Opportunity in Securing Wedding Business

Despite this influx of choice and channels, on the whole, there's an enormous number of venues that are poorly marketed. Many I've met with over the years claim proudly that they only rely on 'word-of-mouth' for their wedding business. Which is a brilliant (and cheap!) means of driving more weddings, but unless word-of-mouth is delivering you the exact number of weddings required each year, solely relying on this form of marketing is a bit like opening a shop three-streets back from the high street: you might be busy, but you could be so much busier.

A common issue we see at DHM with many venues is that the dedicated wedding coordinator is actually only part-time and often is doubled-up in another role within the hotel. This leads to the engaged couples who originally enquired not being followed up properly. With so many venues competing for the attention of the bride/groom-to-be, following up promptly and professionally is a must. Getting this bit right from the offset when the enquiry comes through can give your property the edge.

Probably the biggest opportunity for wedding venues when it comes to standing out and getting noticed is that the online advertising channels of Facebook, Google and Instagram are still widely underused across the industry. Most properties we speak with at DHM aren't using these platforms or aren't using them to their full potential. All too often a hotel will 'boost' a Facebook post without any real targeting or will use Google AdWords without negative keywords. This means that a fair chunk of the boosted Facebook post budget will be spent on people that have no intent nor inclination to find a wedding venue and using Google AdWords without analysing and removing negative keywords is a sure-fire way to keep this platform performing at its most expensive.

(For clarity here: a negative keyword is a search term that you don't want to bid on because you deem it irrelevant for your product. For example, you may wish to bid on the keyword 'wedding venue Surrey' but want to exclude all variations of this that include the word 'cheap' to discourage the wrong type of enquiries. Thus, in this example your ad will appear on Google when the term 'wedding venue Surrey' is searched but not for when 'cheap wedding venue Surrey' is searched. The aim here of course is to achieve higher quality clicks and reduce wastage.)

The opportunity for standing out in this crowded wedding market place is huge, not just because of the relatively low standard of marketing implemented by many wedding venues but also because the revenue for a wedding can well exceed £10,000 in many cases, all things included. From a marketing perspective, you can essentially do more and spend more to secure this business. This ultimately opens up the floodgates of marketing opportunities and avenues. There are things you can do to secure wedding business that just wouldn't be viable in attempting to secure a £300 accommodation booking – which is why we created The Wedding Method...

The Wedding Method

The Wedding Method is primarily about getting more of your ideal customers to find, like and engage with your hotel as a suitable venue for their special day. As you'll no doubt realise, no amount of marketing can 'sell' a wedding (unless of course it's a ridiculously low-priced Groupon deal!), rather the aim of marketing for weddings is to achieve two objectives:

a. Secure an enquiry

b. Secure a viewing

Getting an enquiry isn't all that difficult given the excitable nature of newly engaged women (and men in many cases) tends to encourage them to subscribe to dozens of wedding venues at once with no real intent behind their moderate interest. What's more challenging is securing a wedding viewing: actually getting both halves of the couple to view and experience the hotel with a guided show-around from the wedding coordinator. When a couple commits to travelling to the venue for a pre-arranged viewing appointment, the venue moves from having vague interest to genuine intent. That's the core aim of The Wedding Method.

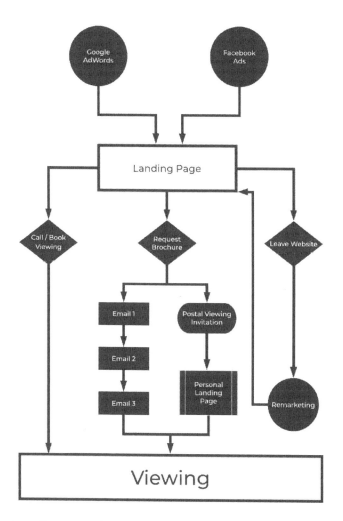

As the diagram illustrates, The Wedding Method is about targeting relevant traffic using Facebook Ads and Google AdWords to a landing page that sits off of your main website. Once on that landing page, the wedding browser has three options:

1. call or book a viewing

2. leave

3. request a brochure for more information

Choosing option one leads them directly to the wedding coordinator for that viewing. This almost never happens first time. Option two: leaving the website will prompt a 540-day remarketing campaign to stay front of mind and entice the wedding browser back to reconsider. Option three means we acquire the wedding browser's contact information which prompts an automatic follow-up process in two ways:

a. a fully automated email auto-responder from the wedding coordinator providing more information

b. a brochure and personalised invitation sent in the post to the wedding browser. This accompanying invitation encourages the user to visit a special website that has been set up which will have their name in the domain: www.yourwebsite.com/sarahsmith When on that page the wedding browser (Sarah Smith in this case) is greeted by a welcoming message 'Welcome Sarah' and invited to choose her preferred wedding viewing times.

This funnel works to shout above all of the noise of all other wedding venue marketing that is on the radar of the wedding browser because – as simple as it may sound – it's really hard to ignore marketing when it has your name on it! Not only will you achieve the necessary cut-through required, you'll also have positioned your hotel as a business that is prepared to go the extra mile. For the wedding browser who receives this marketing it can evoke the feeling that the hotel really cares about their wedding and they've not been treated like just another enquirer.

Whilst this funnel has proven itself time and time again across hotels of all shapes and sizes from the south coast of England to the highlands of Scotland, the way it is implemented matters most to its success. Eighties pop sensations Bananarama said it best: 'It ain't what you do, it's the way that you do it, that's what gets results.' In this part of the book, you'll learn how to implement The Wedding Method in a way that will guarantee a healthy stream of high-quality wedding leads ready to view and book your hotel for their big day.

Take our online assessment now to understand how your wedding marketing rates on our hotel marketing scale. Visit www.thedirectmethod.com

Chapter 14

The Wedding Method:
Relevant Content

The tools available for hotels to get in front of the right wedding browsers have increased dramatically in recent times. Attracting these engaged couples who are actively searching for their dream wedding venue to your website can be typically achieved by one of four means:

Organic traffic

Wedding directory websites

Facebook Ads

Google AdWords

Organic Traffic

These are the wedding browsers that find you naturally on search engines like Google and Bing. To achieve a high position on these websites for search terms like 'wedding venues Oxfordshire' often requires a considerable amount of time, effort and investment into Search Engine Optimisation (SEO). By the way, the above search term features only four wedding venues and six directory websites on page one when typed in on Google. When you consider that over 90% of activity happens on page one of Google, and there are literally hundreds of wedding venues in Oxfordshire, acquiring enough organic traffic direct from the search engines just won't be sufficient for the volume of enquiries needed. Now I'm not discouraging a good SEO strategy, far from it, but as discussed in previous chapters more traffic is not the be-all and end-all of marketing. Additionally, as illustrated in the above example; top rankings for popular keywords are for the tiny minority, so it shouldn't be the only way you're aiming to get relevant traffic to your website.

Wedding Directory Websites

Websites like Hitched are brilliant at helping your hotel or wedding venue to reach a wider audience. These directories help wedding browsers to find quirky venues that they would otherwise not have found and find inspiration from interesting wedding themes and ideas to help them shape their special day. The problem is that these sites are a busy high street of competition where it's not uncommon for a wedding browser to subscribe to 20 or 30 venues in one sitting. As a hotel, these websites undoubtedly give your property exposure, but the relevance of the subsequent website traffic and the enquiries can be questionable. And let's face it, 10 quality, highly-engaged, strong-intent wedding browsers are often better than 100 'leads' that only had to click a 'request more info' button on a directory website. By the time they receive this information and have time to review it, your venue is just one in a pot of dozens. Once again, I'm not advocating not using these websites, but rather have them as part of a larger strategy. The suitability of the traffic and enquiries you receive will, on the whole, probably not be that great, which is why pay-per-click (PPC) advertising should be your best route to market for wedding business.

Facebook Ads

Arguably no platform on the planet gives you better targeting potential than by advertising through Facebook. Astonishingly most hotels who do advertise on this platform typically just boost posts to their Facebook likes and their friends, yet the level of detail one can go into far exceeds this. At DHM, when we set up a Facebook Ad, we first draw a radius of normally around 30-40 miles from the hotel, depending on the population density of the location. When doing this, it's important to only target people who live in this radius, not those who simply happen to be within it. If your hotel is located in a particularly touristic area then it will be important to target your ads only to locals, especially during the summer months of the year.

The next thing we'd do is target people within this radius that have become engaged only in the last three or six months. Facebook predominantly knows this selection of people by the relationship status change, moving from 'in a relationship' to 'engaged'. Depending on the type of venue, price of packages and location, you may choose to narrow these criteria even further by only targeting people who are educated to degree level or above which may suggest a higher level of income and as such more money to spend on the wedding – I'll caveat this with it being a sweeping generalisation and it's certainly not a suitable filter for every hotel.

These ads will now be targeted to people who match these criteria and appear in a multitude of ways across both Facebook and Instagram. There are approx. 12 different ways to advertise on Facebook including paying for impressions rather than clicks, optimising for sign ups and driving straightforward traffic to a website. We almost always prefer the latter: getting wedding browsers away from the attention-grabbing world of social media and onto your own website (or landing page) is a far better way to get maximum interaction and engagement with your hotel.

It's at this point that the split-testing starts. Using a tool like AdEspresso is a very clever way of maximising your budget on Facebook and Instagram. Our philosophy at DHM is very much about using proven marketing principles to drive more business and letting the data guide how to best use these principles. In this context, we know that advertising on Facebook in this way (principle) can work incredibly well; what won't be known is the best headline, image and supporting text to achieve the best results with the least amount of spend (data). To that end, we split-test. Setting up wedding ads in this way will start with choosing five headlines, five images and five supporting sections text for the ads. That gives us 125 different combinations of ads (5 x 5 x 5 = 125) and whilst we might have a good idea which image or which headline or which section of descriptive text will perform best, we have no idea until we test them. To that end, AdEspresso allows us to run all 125 combinations of ads simultaneously to our target audience, being fed equal impressions.

For more information about AdEspresso visit
www.dhm.agency/suppliers

After a few days or a week (depending on the allocated daily budget) there will be clear winners. Typically, we'll choose the five best performing ads from the 125 variations tested and lead with those. Doing this testing work upfront ensures that you are reducing wastage and keeping cost to a minimum from the very start of your campaign.

The other useful thing that Facebook Ads allows you to do is target wedding browsers that fit into certain niches. Same-sex weddings can be targeted by changing the sexual orientation of your intended audience and then changing the ads to match those customers with headlines like 'Same-sex wedding specialists'. Similarly, late availability weddings can be targeted by simply changing the headline to something like 'Looking to tie the knot this year?' and the supporting copy to 'There's a handful of wedding availability dates still remaining for this year! If you're looking to move quickly on your big day, enquire below.' When advertising on Facebook with the objective of acquiring traffic to your website or landing page, these ads are charged on a pay-per-click basis so what you're doing here is to make it very clear that your ad will only be of interest to the individual if their requirement matches the content of the ad. This approach is also useful when wishing to target an older clientele for second or third weddings. Often a simple tweak in the targeting to only appear to people aged 40+, combined with appropriate ad content can help achieve this.

Google AdWords

At DHM, when working with a client to implement The Wedding Method, in most cases we tend to allocate most of the budget to Google AdWords, targeting people who search relevant keywords on Google e.g. 'wedding venue Somerset'. One of the reasons for this is that by virtue of the fact that the wedding browser is actively typing what they're looking for into Google, it gives us a good indication of their intent. Compare this to a platform like Facebook where we know we'll be targeting the right people, but we have no idea on what stage of the decision process the wedding browser is at. For example, a 25-year-old woman who was proposed to yesterday could see an ad on Facebook, click and request more information, despite the fact that she's probably not going to be in a position to *actively* start looking for another six months. Contrastingly, the 31-year-old male who sees the ad on Facebook, clicks and requests more information may actually have already secured his wedding venue; he just does so to compare and find validation that he got a deal!

Therefore, Google AdWords targeting is the process of turning up in front of people who have instigated the wedding venue search themselves, whereas Facebook Ads allows you to turn up in front of people who you think *might* be interested in buying. It's a subtle but significant difference.

Similar to Facebook targeting, Google AdWords allows you to target geographically. You can do this in two ways:

a. Including or omitting certain areas from where the search is made.

b. Including the broad or specific location within the keyword you are bidding on.

For example, you may wish to target your ads to people that are searching for 'wedding venue Somerset' but only within the UK, thus someone who searches this in Singapore will not see your ad.

Longtail keywords can also be targeted to keep the cost-per-click (CPC) down. A longtail keyword is an elongated search term such as 'I'm looking for a wedding venue in Somerset with an amazing view'. The CPC will be lower for these types of keywords as the search volume is much lower, as is the demand from other advertisers.

Niche or specific-interest targeting is also possible within Google AdWords. Some examples could be:

'quirky wedding venues Somerset'

'wedding venue Somerset with a spa'

'converted barn wedding venue Somerset'

'small wedding venue Somerset'

If your wedding venue in Somerset has a spa or is a little quirky the top two keywords in this list would be ideal to bid on. However, this is where a huge amount of wastage happens because setting up an ad to target a 'broad match' and/or a 'phrase match' variation of the keyword 'wedding venues Somerset' would ensure that your ad appeared and was clicked on by all or most of these niche keywords, yet your hotel may be neither quirky, have a spa, be a converted barn nor particularly small. These wedding browsers who would have clicked your ads would quickly realise that your hotel is not suitable for them, and probably bounce right off the website. And when one considers that all of these keywords could cost as much as £2 or £3 per click, if the campaigns aren't managed correctly there won't be much in the way of success.

When managing these campaigns, the core aim is to keep the cost-per-enquiry to its lowest. If each click costs £1 and 1-in-10 clickers converted into an enquiry, your cost-per-enquiry (often called cost-per-lead or CPL for short) would be £10. The work that DHM does (and has won awards for!) is managing these AdWords campaigns to ensure that the cost-per-click and the cost-per-enquiry reduces over time.

Landing Page

When most hotels decide to use Google AdWords or Facebook Ads to attract relevant traffic, they are normally redirected from these Google or Facebook ads onto the wedding page of the hotel's main website. Whilst this might seem logical, it's a really bad idea. When paying significant amounts of money (anywhere between 50p and £3) for each click, you mustn't treat these users like everyone else on the website, allowing them to roam freely across the website to see if it's of interest to learn more. As has been discussed in other chapters, web browsers are fickle and get distracted easily. Whilst they may have searched for something specifically relating to weddings on Google, clicked on your ad and been redirected to the wedding page, they may (and often do) ignore this path and click straight to the homepage, then the image gallery, then the restaurant page and then they leave, never to return.

Of course, that won't be the path chosen by every wedding browser you encourage to your website using PPC ads. When you are paying for a particular wedding browser to consider you for a wedding, it's important that they actually spend time looking at the area of your business that you are paying for them to look at!

To that end, when running PPC ads, at DHM we never drive to a website – always to a landing page that looks similar to the website, but only with information about hosting a wedding at the hotel and absolutely no navigation/menu-bar that will serve to distract the wedding browser away from the job at hand.

Without this landing page approach, all you're doing is spending good money on ads and leaving it to chance. At £2 per click I'd rather not take that chance and make sure that their next steps are limited in choice:

1. Call or book a viewing

2. Request a brochure

3. Leave the website

We'll always make sure there is a unique tracking number in place, so we can track if any of those clicks turn into a direct viewing. If they request a brochure then we have some or part of their contact information that can be followed up, and if they leave we can now remarket to them across the Google Display Network for free for 18 months.

Limiting the options by using a landing page of this nature, you effectively control what the wedding browser experiences and therefore boost your chances of converting them into an enquiry or a viewing.

Chapter 15

The Wedding Method:
Impressive Content

Photography

When searching for the perfect wedding venue, wedding browsers will inevitably visit a multitude of hotel and wedding venue websites during their research process, and during the initial phase of this research, photography is the most important first step. If upon first impression the wedding photography showcased to the wedding browser is not impressive, the chances of them going to the next phase to learn more about the hotel is highly unlikely.

This imagery absolutely must be bespoke. Using stock or generic wedding imagery either involving stunningly beautiful models or generic close-up shots of wedding décor is a bad idea for a couple of reasons:

1. My team and I have, over the years, researched many hotels to get ideas of what looks great and what doesn't. There are a handful of models, mostly female, that turn up regularly during our research process. As soon as a wedding browser

starts to see the same beautiful bride in more than one place, the venue can lose all credibility.

2. Generic décor shots, artistically showing a table set for a wedding, or a close-up shot of a wine glass and a table name; these may look great, but these stock images say nothing about what makes your venue different and once again, there is every chance that your wedding browser has seen the exact same image on another venue's website. If nothing else these images make your hotel look unauthentic which is not the impression you want to give to someone looking to spend in excess of £10,000 with you.

At the risk of labouring the point, as mentioned in previous chapters the imagery you use to promote your hotel must be of the highest quality. That means no iPhone shots and well-lit, professionally produced imagery that looks impressive.

There should be a good combination of empty shots depicting the décor and dressed rooms for a wedding, as well as shots that are full of life. Your wedding browsers don't just want to see empty beautifully presented rooms, they want to see vibrant scenes with friends and families laughing together. Remember that the very purpose a wedding browser is on your website or your landing page in the first place is to understand whether they can envisage their big day in your hotel and perfectly captured moments from real weddings can really help to create that picture in the wedding browser's mind.

This photography should obviously be featured on your website, wedding landing pages and across your social media pages but don't stick to just wedding shots – more often than not a stunning exterior shot can serve you much better than the inside of a room that looks similar to the dozen other venues the wedding browser has already visited.

Finally, one of the most important images you should have is a happy, smiley headshot of your wedding coordinator. Encouraging enquiries and viewings is just as much about the person who they can entrust their wedding to as it is about the building they choose to have it in. This is one of the most important buying experiences of people's lives and it's essential that you make the people as much of a part of this process as the property itself.

Videography

Similar to previous chapters, when it comes to wedding videography the same principles apply; the following three types of video are needed to impress the wedding browser:

1. Showcase videos

2. Testimonial videos

3. Wedding Coordinator interview videos

To showcase the property, you ideally want a multitude of real life weddings edited into series of showcase videos that can sit on your landing pages. As before, they should be shorter than two minutes in length and should bring to life the idea of having a wedding at your hotel in the wedding browser's mind.

Testimonial videos are probably the most important video type when it comes to convincing wedding browsers to engage with your hotel further. Ideally you want bride and groom on the day talking about how special their day has been and how the staff couldn't have done more to make the day so brilliant. If getting footage on the day proves tricky, an interview with the bride and groom before their big day can suffice. Social proof in this context is so important as it offers validation to the wedding browsers that they should take the next step. Also, it's the only thing that can successfully and authentically sell the people in your hotel. Whilst your stunning photography will undoubtedly be able to sell the venue, the people who will make their wedding truly special (your staff) have to be 'sold' via video by your customers.

Lastly, interviews with the wedding coordinator can be really useful in galvanising the wedding browser's intent to learn more about your hotel. Having this person within your business talk openly and passionately about what to expect at the viewing appointment and what they do personally to ensure that every aspect of the wedding is crafted to the individual's needs can be a powerful and influential tool in your conversion process.

Moreover, this type of video would have been seldom seen by your wedding browser throughout their research of other hotels so can serve to give you that important point of difference needed to stand out in the wedding browser's mind.

Chapter 16

The Wedding Method: Data Capture

Two-Step Forms

Over recent years, web browsers have become more reluctant to part with their contact information. It can seem like every company on the Internet wants to get you to click on their ad and have you part with your contact information, so they can send you a never-ending barrage of emails and follow-up communications.

To that end, it's more important than ever to use impressive content (photography and videography) along with clever tools to encourage that web browser to part with their contact information. In recent times, at DHM we have found that a two-step form can facilitate this process.

In essence, a two-step form breaks down the data input process for wedding browsers. The best-case scenario after a newly engaged bride-to-be has clicked on an ad is for her to part with her name, email, full postal address, telephone number and when she's looking to get married. The problem is that whilst this information will be extremely useful for the hotel, it's a lot of information to ask on the first time a wedding browser has come into contact with your business. A two-step form can overcome this by asking only for email and first name on the page. Upon entering this information and clicking on the 'Request Brochure' or 'Submit' button, the wedding browser is kept on the same page but the form changes to ask for a little more information. Normally we'd have the copy changed to 'Enter your address below and we'll pop a copy of the brochure in the post for you, along with a little something extra...' The key benefit of using this approach is that even if they don't go the extra step of adding in their postal information, you will still acquire their name and email.

Split-Testing Lead Magnets

A lead magnet is the term that describes the incentive used to encourage the browser to part with their information. As a general rule at DHM we start with 'request a brochure' when working with a new client as it offers a fine balance between pre-qualifying the wedding browser but not asking for too much commitment too soon. If, for example, we were to ask the wedding browser to book a viewing on the first interaction with your hotel, this would be a bit like proposing on a first date; it's too much too soon. Over the years we have also played around with 'check availability' as a suitable lead magnet, encouraging the wedding browser to enter their contact information and their preferred wedding season, but on the whole 'request a brochure' performs best. As mentioned in previous chapters, almost everything we do at DHM is split-tested, and in this instance, it would not be uncommon for our team to send traffic to three or four different variations of landing pages with different lead magnets to understand what best converts more browsers into enquirers. The tool we use to do this is Instapages which is a landing page builder with brilliant functionality.

For more information about Instapages, visit www.dhm.agency/suppliers

Chapter 17

The Wedding Method: Personalised Follow-up

Email Auto-Responders

So far you have set up some targeted Facebook Ads and Google AdWords, and driven that traffic to a variety of landing pages with stunning photography and videography in the hope of capturing some key data from wedding browsers who want to learn more about your hotel. When those email addresses start coming in, they should be synchronised to your email platform where an email auto-responder is triggered.

At DHM our preferred email solution is Active Campaign due to its reasonable pricing, multitude of features and easy integration with hundreds of tools (like Instapages for example).

> For more information about why we like Active Campaign, visit www.dhm.agency/suppliers

An email provider like Active Campaign allows you to create email auto-responders (also referred to as drip campaigns) which are automatic emails broadcast to your new wedding leads at precise moments in time. Our general strategy for this is as follows:

1. Upon email submission: Introduction email

2. 3 days later: What to expect from your viewing

3. 10 days later: Testimonial

4. 40 days later: Call to action follow-up one month later

5. 100 days later: Call to action follow-up two months later

Email 1 is an opportunity for the wedding coordinator to introduce himself/herself and explain a little about the hotel and its facilities. This email must be aligned to the lead magnet that the wedding browser signed up with, so if they requested a brochure on the landing page the corresponding email must contain the brochure. There should also be a call to action to click a link/reply/call a tracking number to book a viewing.

Email 2 sent three days later contains a testimonial both written and ideally a still of a video with a big play button in the middle, prompting the recipient to click and be redirected to a page to view the video and also book an appointment for a viewing.

Email 3 sent one week on from email 2 normally asks the recipient overtly if they would like to book a viewing and perhaps what that viewing will entail (perhaps a glass of champagne and a show-around the venue).

Emails 4 and 5 simply follow-up a month later and then a further two months later, respectively. The copy should be casual and explain that the wedding coordinator hasn't heard from the recipient just yet and would they be interested in learning more. These follow-ups are important because very often the wedding browsers who enquire for more information may have only just become engaged, and in our experience at DHM, most engaged couples don't start looking actively for a wedding venue until 3-4 months after engagement. So, by staying in touch and turning up in their inbox every month or two you can continue to gently follow-up in an unobtrusive manner.

Automation and Behaviour Tracking

Now you might be wondering what happens if the wedding browser responds or books a viewing in the middle of the auto-email responder sequence: will they still continue to receive follow-ups? In general, the answer is no. Active Campaign's automation features allow you to remove a recipient from the campaign midway through if a specific action is taken. For example, if the recipient clicked the link in email 3 and booked a viewing, some code could be placed on the confirmation page which triggers that particular recipient to receive no further requests to book an appointment. Now this isn't an exact science because inevitably the recipient could pick up the phone and book an appointment directly with the wedding coordinator and the digital marketing systems would have no idea. To combat this at DHM one of our account managers liaises with the wedding coordinator regularly to provide an update of any wedding appointments which have been confirmed in the last few days and normally once a week any 'wedding enquirers' that converted to 'wedding viewers' are removed manually.

One of the reasons why we chose Active Campaign as our original email solution against the wealth of options on the market was because of its behaviour tracking and in particular its website tracking. What this means is that by adding some basic code to each page of your hotel's website, you can understand when a wedding browser who has originally enquired returns to your website to find out more. For example, if a wedding browser submits an enquiry in May and proceeds to ignore all communications but arrives back on the website to have another look in September, a notification email can be sent to the wedding coordinator informing them that 'Sarah Smith is looking at the hotel website right now'.

When you consider that all too often a wedding coordinator can be very busy in their main role as well as dealing with dozens of unqualified leads that have come through from the likes of Hitched, it can be difficult to follow-up with every single one. These handy notification emails can help the wedding coordinator to prioritise their time to follow-up with the warmest leads.

Postal Personalisation

Whilst DHM is at its core a *digital* marketing agency, the best results in marketing come when both online and offline methods are used in unison, and so by following up with a consistent message on both the wedding enquirers inbox and their doormat, you can achieve a greater amount of cut-through to stand out amongst the likely two dozen different wedding venues fighting for their attention.

To clarify on this point: when a wedding browser lands on a landing page having clicked on a Facebook or Google ad, and they have completed both steps of the data capture form (first step: name and email, second step: address and phone number), not only does it trigger an automated email campaign, but also an automated postal campaign. If the lead magnet was 'request a brochure' then within a few days a brochure will arrive on their doormat along with a personal invitation to visit a bespoke webpage (this typically looks like a wedding invitation which is always fun to receive!) This bespoke webpage would normally be a separate website link and have the wedding browser's name at the end. For example: www.manorhotelweddings.com/sarahsmith

This is such a powerful way to get your wedding enquirer to engage with your hotel further, mainly because it's really hard to ignore marketing when it has your name on it! Upon landing on this webpage, in this example she would see some supporting copy with the words 'Welcome Sarah!' featured as a headline. Within this page Sarah is invited to use the appointment booking tool to book her wedding viewing which in turn is directed automatically to the wedding coordinator to inform them of the booking. We use a number of preferred tools depending on the calendar being used by the wedding coordinator.

For more information on the appointment tools we use, visit www.dhm.agency/suppliers

Effectively what we're doing here is giving your hotel a distinct advantage by engaging with the wedding browser in multiple ways, in a personal way. Then through the use of an appointment-setting tool we are making it simple and easy for the wedding enquirer to go to the next step. Adopting this level of sophistication with your wedding marketing will put your hotel head and shoulders above your competition when it comes to engaging with and converting wedding sales.

Chapter 18

The Wedding Method: Remarketing

Whilst remarketing has been covered at length earlier in the book, I don't wish to repeat myself by explaining how this clever marketing tool works, nor why it is so important. What is significant is that wedding remarketing code should be set up both on your landing pages and on your wedding pages within your own website. These ads should feed wedding-specific ads to your wedding browsers and should run for the full 540 days. It's especially important to use the maximum cookie duration given wedding venue decisions can take months or even years before the engaged couple is ready to make a decision.

It's also particularly important when running PPC ads given that if you have spent £1, £2 or even £3 on a click to get a wedding browser onto a landing page and they decide to do nothing and leave, you want to maximise the chance of that investment returning by 'following' that wedding browser around for free for the next 18 months. There's every chance they simply got distracted rather than were disinterested in your hotel.

Chapter 19

Getting The Direct Method Working In Your Hotel

The Direct Method is all about the customer. It affirms that by starting with the customer's relationship with the hotel, the message of your marketing and the media through which it is communicated can begin to take shape.

During the decade that I've been working in hotel marketing, my team and I have had huge successes and some big failures too. In developing The Direct Method, we've drawn upon what's worked and what hasn't, as well what used to work well but is no longer as effective. Our analysis always led us back to one question that remains constant: **what does the customer need to see and experience in order for them to take the desired action?**

Inevitably this proved troublesome as every customer is unique, with specific needs that could vary wildly. What we realised is that, irrespective of these different needs, the *relationship* with a hotel can be grouped into clearly defined categories.

The couple who stayed at a hotel two years ago for an enjoyable short break has a very different view and *relationship* with that hotel than the young man who just happened upon that hotel's website a few moments ago looking for a short break for a few months' time. Categorising the 'relationship status' with your hotel can and should steer the choice of message one uses, and on which medium.

Having spent a great deal of time understanding this, it became clear that every potential accommodation customer that comes into contact with your hotel can loosely be categorised as a Prospect or a Browser.

The Prospect Method uses a combination of email marketing, social media and inexpensive online advertising to remind and engage with potential customers who have already been 'sold' on the benefits of the hotel. Whilst they might not be actively searching for a hotel break, by building and nurturing that already strong relationship, and by creating an enticing buying environment you can move a Prospect from a feeling of indifference about your hotel to one of active consideration.

The Browser Method at its core is about *convincing* customers who are actively looking for a hotel break that your hotel is the right choice and that booking direct is best. This convincing process rarely happens quickly. Stunning imagery and videography help the Browser to form an opinion, inexpensive ads remind and reiterate that opinion, social proof starts to validate that opinion and by creating a smooth browsing experience, a hotel can encourage the Browser to the booking pages. When met with a high-perceived value rate on a simple and slick booking engine the Browser will likely be inclined to book.

The Wedding Method uses clever online ad targeting to get in front of people who are highly likely to be looking for a wedding venue that matches your product. It combines innovative digital techniques with traditional marketing methods to surprise and delight with an unexpected level of personalisation. Implemented effectively, this personal touch makes a hotel stand out in a crowded market place and works not to sell the 'wedding', but rather to sell the 'wedding conversation'. To put it another way, it does the heavy lifting upfront so that engaged couples arrive at the hotel pre-sold.

The development of the two accommodation methodologies is the result of a continual belief that over-reliance on third party agents, (be it OTAs, deal websites or any other third party) is unnecessary for hotels and that there is another, better way to acquire business. Similarly, The Wedding Method was created with the belief that by having your marketing evoke positive feelings of trust and delight within a well-crafted funnel can dramatically improve visibility and perception of your hotel in a crowded market place.

When implemented effectively, The Direct Method is an empowering strategy that can breathe life back into a cash-strapped hotel business and reignite the passion of a frustrated hotelier who has become victim of lower rates and higher overheads. At DHM, it's one of my true pleasures in business to watch and experience this transformation. My hope is that The Direct Method provides you the impetus to take action and I wish you every success on that path to growing your business.

Let's beat those OTAs together.

> To take our free online assessment of how your hotel could drive more direct accommodation bookings and increase weddings, go to www.thedirectmethod.com

92383333R00077

Made in the USA
Lexington, KY
03 July 2018